In Christ
Margaret Johnson

18,
No Time to Waste.

Kathi

FRANK
MORTON

18,

No Time to Waste

Margaret
Johnson

Illustrations by Frank Morton

ZONDERVAN PUBLISHING HOUSE
A Division of The Zondervan Corporation
GRAND RAPIDS, MICHIGAN

EIGHTEEN . . . NO TIME TO WASTE

© 1971 by Zondervan Publishing House
Grand Rapids, Michigan

Library of Congress Catalog Card Number 71-157400

Second printing March 1972
Third printing October 1972

Printed in the United States of America

For
Kathi

To
Felicia
Sharon
Brad
Jon
And in special memory of Jim.

My thanks to my cousin, Dr. John Edmund Haggai, who first encouraged me to tell Kathi's story.

My special thanks to Ethel Emily Wallis for her invaluable advice and many hours of reading and organizing the manuscript. Without her, this book could not have been written.

Tears will always fill my eyes when I think of the skinny, dark-haired girl who flew in and out of our home, who filled our lives with havoc, fun, some heartbreak, lots of noise, and finally with a great sense of pride and joy. I will always anticipate that great moment when the curtain goes down on this life and lifts for a brighter and more glorious one — when we shall be reunited with her.

Coming years will bring other pleasures, other heartaches, and other losses, and as the years pass, the memory of Kathi will fade a little, as it must. But whatever the future holds, Kathi will always have been the one who taught me the most about being a mother, about being a Christian, about being a witness — about being a friend.

"Thank you, Kathi."

18.
No Time to Waste.

1

"MOM, THERE'S SOMETHING I want to talk to you about. Now don't say 'no' until you hear me out."

I watched Kathi, now almost eighteen years old, as she made meaningless patterns on the tablecloth with her fork, her eyes downcast. A feeling of fear rose in my throat and caused me to stiffen.

"It's this, mom; Felicia and I want to get an apartment together for the summer —

"— just for the summer," she added hastily, as she lifted her head and saw my face.

"You know the answer to that; it's *no*. I won't even discuss it," I said with fierce finality.

I got up from the table and walked away, hoping to close the subject once and for all. Kathi didn't move.

"You've got to see it my way, mom. It's something I want to do, just for the summer. I promise I'll be back in the fall — please, just *listen* to me!"

All of the "How to rear your children" advice came back to me and bounced off my brain with a painful thud. Tears were threatening to break through at any moment, and I hardly dared trust my voice to answer. I stood there looking at my second daughter, her usually happy face now stricken. I knew that I could change that by one

11

sentence, "Yes, go, Kathi, with my blessing." But I couldn't say words I didn't mean.

Kathi, at seventeen, was a slender girl with raven-colored hair that fell long and loose about her face. Just under her bangs were dark, luminous eyes, quick to reveal her every mood. She vibrated with life and energy, her vivacity drawing people to her. She was like a magnet to the teen-agers who were constantly around her. She seemed to give so much of herself that her friends were seeking her out for the sheer pleasure of her company. It had always been like this. I don't know why I hadn't gotten accustomed to it by this time, but it still irritated me to have to always vie for her time. But Kathi was Kathi! Her friends were numerous.

But Felicia was a special friend!

And I didn't like Felicia!

As Kathi and I stood there facing each other, what I really felt was anger: Anger built up in me toward Felicia who had taken Kathi from me; anger toward her friends who had more of her than I did.

And I was angry at the wall that had built up between us. Everyone always told me Kathi was different, Kathi was special, and yet I, her mother, was having the hardest time understanding her. I was angry that she would even want to leave home. Most of all, I was angry that that magic age of eighteen was soon to be hers — and I was helpless to stop her.

"No, no, no!" I heard my own voice saying and could hardly believe it was mine. "You can't leave, and if you do, you can't come back. No."

I brushed past her before the tears erupted into a fountain of grief, ran into the bedroom, and flung myself on the bed.

Kathi stood at my door, struggling to control herself.

"Why? Why do you want me to stay then?" she was asking. "Is it because I'm the only daughter left at home, or because you want me to run errands for you? Why? You have the boys — you don't need me!"

She started to walk away, and I said the only thing I could think to say. I called after her through a voice choked with emotion.

"Because, Kathi — because I love you!"

Kathi was out the front door, and the house was quiet. I lay back on the bed with a heavy heart.

It was early March, and the California breezes were whispering that spring would soon be here. It was nearly dusk, and soon it would be time to prepare dinner for Vern and the boys.

Kathi, my heart cried out, *where did you go?*

When did we build this barrier between us?

Was it long ago when you were just a little girl and I was having baby after baby and you were made to grow up so fast?

Was it when your older sister Cindy became a teenager and she and I shared so many secrets together?

Was it when Cindy was married and you felt that "second daughter" jealousy?

Was it resentment that you had now become big sister to a brood of noisy brothers?

What had happened to the chubby little five-year-old who took my hand and gently asked me to help her pray "for Jesus to come into my heart"?

I sobbed quietly, praying between sobs that God would help me know how to bridge the gap between us. I was sure that Kathi was driving off to Sharon's or Felicia's to share this new confrontation with them. Kathi, Sharon, and Felicia had become an inseparable threesome, silly and irresponsible. I suppose Kathi shared the attitude of most teens — "leave me alone."

But I was determined to slow her down, to force her to understand her responsibilities, and in the process, I had met a personality as strong as my own.

And now she was coming of age, and I was heartsick. It seemed only yesterday I had held her in my arms, welcoming my second daughter with real joy.

Vern and I had so wanted to train and teach our chil-

13

dren to love and live for God. But somewhere along the way, I had become rigid and unbending in my views.

"Lord," I prayed, "teach me patience and love and understanding with Kathi."

It was with this resolve that I helped Kathi plan the slumber party for her eighteenth birthday. She was so excited, scrubbing and cleaning the house, running to the store for last-minute items. Her enthusiasm never failed to buoy my own spirits.

As the girls began to arrive and I watched Kathi greeting them at the door, I had to smile. *It's no wonder that everyone loves her so,* I thought. *She greets every girl as if she were the only one in the world.*

I had always loved Kathi's slumber parties, but this night was one I would always remember. The house was soon full of giggling girls, huddling together in the living room, with wall-to-wall sleeping bags, huge rollers sticking out of their hair in every direction. They laughed and screamed long into the night, drinking Cokes, munching potato chips and doughnuts, and capturing their most awkward moments with flash cameras.

And there was Kathi — always the center of attraction, the last one to sleep and the first one up — the perfect little hostess running back and forth with food trailing behind her.

The stereo blasted all the "now" music, and though Vern and I could hardly sleep, we were intoxicated with our daughter's happiness. As I listened to the gaiety that filled the house, I thought, *maybe after graduation Felicia will go with her parents to Texas and the girls will forget their plans for leaving home.* I smiled smugly, comforting myself, but there was a nagging uncertainty deep within me.

The next morning there was the usual aftermath and clean-up. I found Coke bottles under chairs and on tables; empty potato chip bags were scattered about the room,

14

with remnants of chips littering the carpet; doughnut boxes, emptied to the last crumb, were everywhere.

And Kathi was upstairs — sleeping soundly.

As I cleaned the house, I thought, *this is probably the last slumber party Kathi will ever have.*

I was right. It was to be her last slumber party — and her last birthday!

2

KATHLEEN ANNE WAS BORN on a blustery cold March morning in Michigan in 1951. I held her tightly to me, unwrapping the blanket carefully. I had wanted another girl and was delighted when the nurse told me we had a daughter. *Two girls are perfect,* I thought, contentedly, that morning. I had always wished for a sister but had grown up in a houseful of boys. It would be fun to buy dolls for them, to dress them alike, to experiment with hair styles, to buy pretty hair ribbons and barrettes — and tiny patent leather shoes.

Suburban Grand Rapids was a quiet, peaceful place to raise children. We had just purchased our first new home, and we settled down with our two girls to a contented sort of life.

Although my daughters were extremely different, they were both precious to me. Cindy was tiny, with long curly hair that fell into ringlets — a real charmer. Kathi grew chubby and vivacious, always on the go. She was a match for Sheba, the dog who raced around the house with her when she visited Grandma and Grandpa Johnson. She loved to catch the dog by the tail to make him "stop."

From the time she could talk, Kathi chattered with everyone she met. She loved to go visiting, and when she was

17

only four, she was delighted to hear of a trip to California to visit my parents.

"Girls," I told Cindy and Kathi one day in the spring, "we are going way out to California to visit grandpa and grandma, and when we come back, after a little while, you will have a little brother or sister." They danced out of the room, chuckling and giggling.

"Of course, it will be a boy," I told Vern seriously. "That's what we ordered." We were both anxious for a son.

We spent two delightful months with my parents near the ocean in beautiful Pacific Palisades, becoming more and more addicted to the soft sea breezes, the towering mountains, and the temperate climate. Finally, just one month before our son Richard was born, we reluctantly said goodby and took a train back home to the Midwest. Cindy and I sat quietly reading for most of the trip, while Kathi bounced up and down the aisle, meeting and greeting strangers, chattering constantly in her four-year-old gibberish. She was doing what came most naturally to her — making people love her.

From the time Cindy and Kathi were babies, Vern and I had taught them about Jesus and prayed with them. Kathi loved to sing. Always the "ham," she would stand before adult groups and lisp out her songs. One that she loved especially was:

> My desire to be like Jesus
> My desire to be like Him.
> His spirit leads me,
> His love overwhelms me;
> In word and deed, to be like Him.

Kathi was still and thoughtful when she heard the Bible stories and when she prayed. She seemed to understand at an early age what trusting the Lord Jesus meant.

It was late one Sunday afternoon when Kathi was nearing her fifth birthday that she came to me, took my hand, and said clearly, "Mommy, make Cindy leave the room."

"Why, honey?" I asked.

She pulled me down to her and whispered, "Because I want to ask Jesus into my heart."

I motioned for Cindy to leave the room, and Kathi and I knelt by the sofa.

"Dear Jesus," Kathi prayed in her childish voice, "please come into my heart today."

Tears formed quickly in my eyes as I hugged her to me. "Now remember, Kathi, when we ask Jesus into our hearts, He will never leave. He promised to be with us always."

She nodded, and her dancing dark eyes were still and serious. Kathi had made her first commitment to her Lord. It was the first stepping stone on her own private path that would lead her to future commitments and to that very last step.

3

MICHIGAN WAS NEVER THE SAME for us after that trip to California. We had become completely dazzled by the beauty of the coastal town of Pacific Palisades. Going to the beach in April, mowing the lawn in December, and saying good-by to boots and mittens just seemed too good to be true.

So when Vern was offered a job, we left immediately. We bought a tiny house just a few blocks from my parents and settled down to a new way of life.

When Christmas rolled around that year, we all swallowed a lump in our throats, thinking of snowmen, tobogganing, and cozy nights by the fireplace. It took us time to become acclimated to the new "life style" that was California living — but not too long.

Soon we were learning how to "live outdoors," barbecuing in the backyard, and shopping for Christmas presents in summer clothes. Sunglasses were as necessary as the car keys — it seemed a land of perpetual sunshine.

It didn't take us long to accustom ourselves to the bustling, traffic-packed freeways, either. A place was never miles away; it was minutes or hours. We had Disneyland, Knotts Berry Farm, and occasionally a glimpse of a famous personality.

Our fourth child, David, was born the same year we

21

made our home in California, and our prayer for a brother for Richard was answered.

"Just what we ordered." Vern and I were elated. "Two girls and two boys."

I was a little premature in my smugness, however, for David was only nine months old when I felt the old familiar nausea. Rushing to the doctor, I heard the, by now, routine words. "Why yes, Mrs. Johnson, you are going to have a baby."

It was too much, too soon, I thought angrily as I drove home. How in the world would we ever care for five children. Our house was small, our finances smaller, and my strength even smaller.

"I can't believe it," I said for nine months. And even on the way to the hospital, I felt the tiniest resentment that this baby had ruined our best-laid plans.

But when they laid Danny in my arms, all resentment vanished. He was a beautiful, perfect boy. I was sure God had sent him for a special purpose.

However, the "fun" days with the girls were over. Life became a constant routine of baby bottles, diapers, heads to wash, hair to comb, shoes to polish, and endless nights with crying babies. And always I seemed to be saying, "No, no, don't touch . . . don't spill your milk . . . take your nap. . . ."

"These are the best years of your life," people would tell me, and I would nod wearily, never believing it. With three boys just under three, every ounce of energy seemed drained from my body.

The girls were rushed out of the door to school in the morning, their questions left unanswered. In the afternoon after school Cindy found solace in curling up with a book, but Kathi spent more and more time with her friends at their homes. The lines of communication to her were already becoming shaky.

I wanted with all of my heart to keep Kathi close to me, but there seemed to be no time or way. She was independent and found compensation with friends outside our home, which was bulging at the seams with children.

"Let's face it, mom," she told me once, "you had too many kids."

I didn't answer her, but a heavy depression settled on me. Prosperity was everywhere in the Pacific Palisades, except at our house. We were badly needing more room for our growing children.

Los Angeles, with its many suburbs, was sprawling over a large area of Southern California, and places which were once filled with productive orange groves now gave way to tracts of homes or apartment houses. Ranch areas were converted into self-sufficient communities centered around large, complete shopping centers.

Away from the ocean and over the hills lay the San Fernando Valley, one of the fastest growing suburban areas adjacent to Los Angeles. On Sunday afternoon we would take the children for a drive through Topanga Canyon out to the valley, in search of a more adequate house for our family, but within our means.

As we topped the mountain road and headed down into the valley, it was like gazing down upon a vast ocean of houses. We drove through tract after tract, street after street. After looking at many of them, we stepped into one ranch-type house and both said, "This is it." We moved in late summer with our little brood.

It was a long, hot summer in the San Fernando Valley. Crisis after crisis faced our family. I went into the hospital for a routine operation, complications set in, and I found myself back in the hospital for the better part of the summer.

An enormous hospital bill came as a result of that illness. There seemed to be only one solution. I would have to go to work as soon as I regained my strength.

Spring found Cindy seriously ill and in the hospital. Then under doctors' orders she was put to bed for six months. Cindy and I shared a unique closeness because of her illness, and Kathi was beginning to feel left out of things.

We often teased Kathi that she was always the one to hold open the front door while we rushed one of the other children to the doctor.

To me, Kathi seemed indestructible.

I felt that we must make it up to her some way because I had to spend so much time with Cindy and the boys, so Vern and I decided to buy her the puppy she had longed to own.

"I'll take care of her; I'll feed her; I'll clean up after her." Kathi was so excited.

And so Queenie came to live with us — a little black and white bundle of sheer energy that matched Kathi's. They chased each other in the backyard. Queenie snuggled up next to Kathi in the evening, and all the love and affection she had bottled up, she lavished on that little puppy.

Wherever Kathi was, Queenie would be. Often at night I would find Queenie cuddled up in bed with her, hiding under the blankets at the foot of the bed.

One day when a truck turned recklessly down our street and hit the helpless Queenie, killing her instantly, Kathi could not be comforted.

"Do puppies go to heaven, mommy," she asked me, the tears streaming down her face.

I cried with her as we put away Queenie's things. And though I promised to buy her a puppy real soon, Kathi, so sensitive, so tender, was deeply hurt when she lost Queenie.

4

"NOW, KIDS," VERN TOLD the children the same day I had found an office job near home, "mom is going to have to work, and you will all have to share in responsibilities."

Cindy, in high school, was a responsible teen-ager, and I knew she would do exactly as she was told. Kathi was twelve, and we felt she could help with the care of the boys. Danny would be staying with my mother while I worked. It seemed the only answer for a difficult financial problem.

Kathi had so many friends on the block now and so many things to do, it was increasingly difficult for her to remember all the home chores. I found myself wishing that she could be a little more like Cindy, who was gracious, obedient, and quiet. Kathi was a tomboy who loved to wear her daddy's T-shirts and her blue jeans. Her hair grew long and her bangs seemed permanently embedded in her eyes. Oh, the battles that we fought over hair styles. Pleading, scolding, threatening — nothing worked.

"Mom," Kathi approached me one day, "Aileen takes piano lessons, and we could go the same night. Could I?"

"There's nothing I would like better, honey," I told her, "if you promise to practice."

I had always found a deep satisfaction in music — sometimes it seemed my only oasis. Nothing would please me more than to have my children learn to play the piano. I also thought that perhaps we could bridge the gap between us at the piano.

I was wrong! Piano lessons were not for Kathi. She loved to play and sing and make her own arrangements, but practicing was quite another thing. Scales and exercises were a bore. I would sit on the bench to help her and we would both end up in tears.

"That isn't *right*, Kathi," I'd insist. "Now play it over." She would play it over with the same mistake.

"Now listen, this is the way it goes." And I would play the measure for her. "Try it."

"I'm getting tired. I don't want to practice anymore."

"But you have your lesson tonight."

"I know. I'm going to ask if I can play something more popular," Kathi said, and she did.

She brought home the little piece "Tammy," which was so popular at that time, and by the end of the evening was playing it with her own arrangement and flourishes. Poor Mrs. Rubin! She never could understand Kathi. She wanted to teach her how to play the piano, and all Kathi wanted to do was *play*.

Kathi's adolescent years were punctuated with constant reminders by Vern and me about cleaning her room, trips to the dentist to fit her braces, music lessons, with stormy practice sessions, baby-sitting her younger brothers — and those were only a few of the things she tried to avoid.

Where she really wanted to be was at the corner baseball lot, or down the street shooting basketballs, or walking into town with Aileen or Candy, or spending the day in Candy's pool.

We had, out of necessity, moved into a larger home the summer Kathi was thirteen, just a few blocks from her junior high school. All the boys were in school now, and we were depending on the girls for after-school baby-sitting.

"Kathi," Vern would tell her again and again, "come right home after school and watch the boys."

Her dark head nodded in accord. "Sure, daddy."

But there were so many activities attracting her after school, so many places to explore, so many friends to stop and chat with, that often it took her until dinner time to come home.

"I forgot," she would say, her dark eyes all innocence.

By the time dinner was over, dishes done, and homework assignments finished, Kathi was on the phone talking to Sharon or Michele or Nancy about how or where they would meet in the morning, what they would wear, or the latest junior high news. And so it went until the last dregs of night were drawn and Kathi fell into bed.

Kathi's vibrancy vanished in the morning, and getting up was an effort. She was definitely a nocturnal person. She walked through the getting-up process and ate breakfast in a daze, so instructions for the day never seemed to get through at that early hour.

Kathi soon became the neighborhood pet on our new block. She was the baby-sitter and friend to the younger women on the street. They loved her. But it was more than disconcerting to me that her own chores went undone while she helped a neighbor clean up her house or mind her children.

"Vern, you must speak to that girl." She became "that girl" soon after the advent of the television program of the same name. Not only did she resemble the star of the show, but she also had the same exuberant personality. Everyone began calling her "that girl."

Vern had long talks with her in his gentle, understanding way, and she responded to him, promising to keep her room clean, comb her hair, wear her shoes, and come home right after school.

During those stormy years, Vern was always a great help. He and Kathi had a beautiful understanding, and he could reason with her.

"Just leave her alone," he would admonish me. "She'll be all right."

Vern was a strong right arm for Kathi, too, when she

27

began to question the foundations of the faith which she had accepted so fully as a child.

"Dad, how do we know our religion is the right one?" she asked Vern after church one night. Vern took the Bible and sat down at the table with Kathi, patiently outlining verses for her to read and ponder.

"You see," Vern explained, "there was a great gap between God and man because of sin, and there was nothing that could bridge that gap — not being good, not trying harder — nothing. So, God Himself, in the person of Jesus Christ, came to be that bridge. When we have faith in Him, trusting Him for forgiveness of our sins, and ask Him to be Lord of our lives, then God accepts us because of what Jesus did at Calvary for us."

Kathi had more questions as she mingled with teen-agers of other faiths, but Vern, always patient, would help her. She began studying the word of God for herself, and I often found *Living Letters* next to her bed, with verses underlined in red. She was seeking God and seeking answers.

"But what about all the people who have never heard, dad? What about my friends? Isn't being a good person good enough?"

"That's an old question, Kathi, and a good one," Vern answered. "But we can trust God to do what's right and fair. And it's our responsibility to tell everyone, everywhere about Jesus. In other words, to do what He says — to be His witnesses."

One night as I passed Kathi's room, I heard her crying. I opened the door and went in and sat on the edge of her bed.

"What's wrong, honey?"

"It's about God. He just doesn't answer my prayers. I pray and pray and He doesn't answer."

"Ah, but He *will*, honey." I brushed her long hair from her face and kissed her wet cheek. "Sometimes it takes awhile and we become impatient, but God always answers — somehow, some way. I know that from experience."

Kathi was going through the early teen syndrome of finding herself; she was questioning God and questioning herself. It was a phase, I knew, and I was grateful for the moments when she would open up to me and share her problems. She told me about troubles of her friends which weighed upon her. She was deeply concerned for her friends and shouldered their problems as if they were her own.

"You're just too young to cope with everyone's problems, Kathi," I would tell her, but she paid no attention.

Through her struggles, Kathi was finding answers and becoming strong in her faith. She was "tuned in" to God.

Junior high days would soon be over; Kathi was becoming more and more involved with her school friends. For the past few summers she had gone to summer church camps and had been involved with youth activities and meetings in our church. Now that was over.

"I'm not mad at God," she would say. "I just have to have time to *think*."

The days of turmoil between us were just ahead.

5

"BUT I DON'T WANT TO GO," Kathi was protesting loudly. "I can stay here with Cindy. It won't be any fun for me."

We were planning our vacation at Yosemite that year and had decided to rough it. Vern bought a tent and sleeping bags and all the equipment we would need. I couldn't say it was exactly my idea of a relaxing vacation, but I knew the boys would love it. The hot summer days that always invaded the valley from June through October were upon us. It would be a relief to get out of the heat and smog and into clean mountain air.

Now Kathi was pouting, but I was insistent that she go along with us. She was fifteen, and she didn't want to leave her friends for the summer.

"You'll have fun once we get there," we encouraged her, and reluctantly she began packing.

The long trip up into the Yosemite mountains and the boys at their noisy, boisterous ages sent Kathi sinking further and further into the seat of the car.

By the time we finally found a camping spot and had pitched the tent, it was dark.

"Be careful of bears!" our camping neighbors called out.

"Oh?" I said, glancing at Kathi who was afraid of a moth.

We were up early, and Vern had the coffee on the cook-stove while we were dressing. Oh — it was cold. The boys hopping around in their sweatshirts thought this was the biggest adventure of all — eating breakfast outdoors. Kathi was silent.

I thought the week was going to be a complete wash-out for her. But late that afternoon a lovely big trailer pulled up beside us and two teen-age girls jumped out. We felt like veteran campers by now, and so we introduced ourselves and invited them to join us for a barbecue that night.

Kathi started to bubble, effervescent as always. She was back on her own ground with friends her own age. The three of them took off for a hike the next day, and when Kathi came back to camp, she had a boy with her. They were barefoot and holding hands. Her two new girl friends each had a boy in tow also.

"This is Mike, mom and dad," Kathi said casually, as though she had known him all her life.

Kathi was her usual vivacious self. Swimming under the bridge, walking with Mike through wooded lanes, sipping Cokes on the benches, she was all smiles.

"Can this be the same girl we brought up here?" Vern said in astonishment.

We hardly saw her that week. After a hearty outdoor breakfast, off she would go with Mike, and the whole day would pass without a sight of her.

"And I thought it would be different up here," I complained, but not too unhappily. I was glad she was having fun.

Mike was puppy love. Kathi was fifteen, and she had found a boy who liked the same things she did.

"Can't we stay one more day, just one more day?" she begged, with her two girl friends hopping up and down and Mike standing shyly to the side.

"Afraid not, honey," we told her. "We have to get back."

The ride home was a repeat performance; Kathi was silent.

32

Already she was sure she would never see Mike again. "He's going to write to me," she said. "And maybe come to see me sometime."

It didn't take Kathi long after we were home before she was back into the swing of things with her old friends. She and Mike did write faithfully at first, but when he finally came to see her, she had almost forgotten who he was.

Anyway, there were so many other things to think about. Kathi was getting ready for the biggest moment of her life — she was getting ready for high school. All our thoughts and plans now were on that big day when she would start Cleveland High. Most of her junior high friends would be going there, too.

So far I had approved and welcomed Kathi's friends, but soon I was to reverse that decision.

I was about to meet Felicia!

"Mom, this is Felicia," she said that November, and it was as though she were saying, "This is someone special."

"She doesn't go to Cleveland," Kathi continued. "I met her at the Y-Club; she goes to St. Genevieve High School."

It was sometime later that I found what Kathi had written about the beginning of her friendship with Felicia. It was a composition for her English class entitled "Some Important Thing That Happened to Me This Year."

September, 1966, I entered high school with high goals and meaningful aims. By October, 1966, I hated school and by November I couldn't wait to graduate. During November I met a friend who asked me to join a Y-Club, and thinking this meant instant popularity, I joined. It turned out that at that time, it was the right thing to do.

Well, to make a long story short, I met another friend who today is my best friend, and this story is about her. As I tell how we became friends, and what we've accomplished, I don't expect anyone to understand. I am writing this mainly because I think we are great.

As I walked into that first club meeting, the first person I saw was Felicia, her big ears hanging out. You might wonder why I mention that fact, but that is actually how we became friends. I ran up to her and yelled, "You have big ears, too!" Well, when she saw mine, we both started laughing and haven't stopped since.

It was instant friendship, and we began plotting and planning immediately. We were out to conquer the world and in our way of thinking we have. The first thing we did proved that we were going to get away with murder. Felicia spent the night with me and we decided to sneak out about midnight. (It was difficult as we have a two-story house, and my room is on the second floor.) We got out and went over to some new houses that were being built and looked around the rooms. This started our expeditions.

We messed around all that semester until it was time for summer vacation. Summer '67 was the greatest time of my life. I learned a lot about people and life in general, and it didn't matter if I was popular. We both quit the club, which we felt wasn't for us, and started doing what we wanted to do. We went to the beach a lot and met new people.

As the summer passed and school began, we had to think of ways to cut classes; we used many methods, and they all worked. One day when we were at my house, Felicia's mother called and caught us, and that was the end of cutting classes for awhile.

This is only a few things we've done, but after high school we plan to take a trip. And after that, who knows what?

I don't know what grade Kathi got on her short essay, but I would give her an "A" for accuracy. She and Felicia

34

were constantly thinking up new ways to be together, whether by car or by telephone.

"I don't like Felicia," I told Vern one day. "I wish Kathi would find some friends from church."

Felicia was a tall, rather sedate girl, lovely, really, with long, dark hair. She was an introvert who complemented Kathi's outgoing personality. I knew I was being hasty and unreasonable in my judgment of Felicia, but I had taken my stand and wouldn't back down.

"I just don't like her, Kathi," I said over and over. "She seems — well — unhappy."

"Felicia is my best friend, mom," Kathi countered.

"I still don't like her," and I felt a tightening in my chest as Kathi walked away. The gap between us widened.

"I don't understand Kathi," I complained to Vern that night. "She loves her friends more than she does us. She always has something going with them."

"The storm will pass, honey," Vern assured me. "She'll grow out of it." But the clashes between us became more frequent. . . .

"Kathi, you should have Christian friends from church."

"You're wrong, mom," she contradicted in her direct manner. "If all my friends were believers in Christ, how could I win them to the Lord?"

I couldn't argue with her logic, but I was afraid, thinking of all the possibilities of temptations that could confront her. I saw Kathi as impulsive and willing to try anything once. I didn't know that my strong-willed daughter was actually standing her ground for Christ, never backing down from her convictions.

Kathi was dating Tom, a boy of another faith. Everyone in the family liked Tom; he was artistic, pleasant, and had a contagious sense of humor. But Tom was as adamant in his faith as Kathi was in hers, and often their dates would end in arguments or debates about each other's faith, until Kathi brought a halt to their dating.

"I could never marry a boy of another faith," she told me.

Of all the friends, and especially boyfriends, who were drawn to Kathi, I believe it was John who really adored her. John had graduated from Kathi's high school and was attending U.C. Riverside on a football scholarship. He seemed to fit right in with our family, and we all admired him.

There wasn't anything that Kathi would ask for that John didn't try his hardest to get for her. Once she mentioned that she would love to have a birthstone ring. Before the words were hardly out of her mouth, John presented her with a tiny blue birthstone ring. Kathi wore it constantly, even after she had broken off with John and was dating others.

But Kathi couldn't date a boy for long without telling him of her love for the Lord Jesus Christ and what her faith meant to her. Soon John was accompanying Kathi to our church services, wanting to find out for himself what she was talking about.

I was at the piano on that special Sunday morning when John slipped past Kathi and walked down the aisle in response to Pastor Smith's invitation to receive Christ as Savior. Jim Wallis, a missionary home on furlough from Brazil, took John into the church study to talk with him. That day Kathi had led her first friend to Jesus Christ.

Even Felicia, brought up strictly in another faith, listened to Kathi tell about Christ. And on a Sunday not too long after John's conversion, Felicia, too, walked down that aisle. She was the second of Kathi's friends who had a personal encounter with Christ because of her witness.

6

THE SPRING OF KATHI'S JUNIOR year we learned
that my dad had leukemia and would probably live for six
months, at the most. We were saddened as we sat at my
parents' table on Mother's Day, for we all knew these were
his last days with us. Dad sat at the head of the table, as
always, full of conversation about his wonderful Lord. Dad
was the head of the house in every sense, the glory in the
home. It would be so empty without him.

All of the family sat about him, my brother and his
children and all our children — except Kathi. When we had
finished eating and were relaxing over dessert and coffee,
in breezed Kathi with John behind her.

"What's to eat, grandma?" she exclaimed, greeting her
grandpa with a kiss. And John and Kathi sat down with
"oh's" and "ah's" as grandma, always quick to serve her
grandchildren, brought them delicious food.

"I like that girl," dad said quietly to me. "She's not
afraid of anything. She's my girl." His eyes were shining.

And the feeling was mutual; Kathi loved her grandpa. A
few weeks later as he lay dying in the hospital, she stood
at the foot of his bed.

"Grandpa," she said, with tears in her eyes, "I just led
my two best friends to Christ."

"That's wonderful, honey," he smiled weakly. "Keep up
the good work."

I stood there looking at them, thinking how alike they were — both so dynamic in their witness for Christ.

We buried dad in early June, and after the service I overheard Kathi talking to a weeping friend of the family.

"Don't grieve for my grandpa; he's with the Lord." And then she proceeded to tell her how she could know for sure that she would go to heaven.

Sometime later I read in Kathi's diary: "I want to be just like grandpa. I want to tell everyone, everywhere about Jesus."

I have often heard that fathers have a special way with daughters, and this was certainly true in our case. Vern understood Kathi and always told her how proud he was of her, and she justified all of his pride.

She was like "the first star you see at night," twinkling in an otherwise starless sky, making everyone aware of its brightness. She made you feel that she could scale any mountain, dare anything, do anything. She was voted by her high school friends as "the girl you'd most like to be on a desert island with."

Kathi loved everyone — old people, handicapped children, aunts, uncles, cousins, grandmas and grandpas — they were all quick to warm to her affection. The only people she couldn't tolerate were those she labeled "phonies, not real," and she bristled at the slightest hint of it.

"I will do my own thing. I won't be a phony," she'd say. "Accept me for me. I'm not Cindy. I'm me!"

When she helped teach the children in summer Bible school, the little tots, even the shyest ones, would clamor for Kathi. She had a way with children, as evidenced by the little ones knocking at the door calling for her. Out she'd go to take Dede or Kevin for a walk, or she'd run across the street to play with the new baby. I might as well have tried to hold a wisp of smoke in my hands as to hold Kathi back.

But I was trying to shift gears and accept the whirlwind of activity, the flying feet, and the independent ways which surrounded her.

7

"IT SOUNDS AS THOUGH the house is falling down."
I stopped in the middle of the room and listened.

"It's just Kathi," Vern said with a smile. "She's at it
again."

Upstairs she was practicing frantically for cheerleader
tryouts, and her bedroom was directly over ours. Vern
didn't seem to mind, but her endless jumping bothered me,
and I knew the mess it was creating. I was tired of forever
picking up those little bits of paper that flew in all direc-
tions from the pompons which she shook with frantic enthusiasm.

Now Kathi was bounding down the stairs, two at a time.
Her legs, long and slender, moved gracefully under her red
and white cheerleading skirt.

"Watch me, mom! Look —" She was breathless, and
her dark eyes were bright with excitement. Then she twirled
and swirled in every possible position, her tiny frame one
continuous vibration.

"Is it jerky? Is it smooth? Does it look good? Is it
smooth enough do you think?" She looked at me hopefully,
and without waiting for my answer, she was up in the air
again, her dark hair flying in every direction. I smiled in
spite of myself at my second daughter, putting her whole
vivacious self into tryouts.

"I'll never make it," she sat down, suddenly discouraged. "There are so many girls trying out."

"You'll make it," I said, and Vern echoed my words.

"Kathi, you'll not only make the cheerleading team; you'll be head of them all," Vern encouraged her.

She smiled at us uncertainly and went on with her practicing.

"She's doing what comes naturally for her," I told Vern later that night. "Jumping, bouncing, smiling, cheering . . . that's Kathi."

"Then why can't you accept her for what she is?" There was a hint of rebuke in his words, and I quickly rose to my own defense.

"I just wish she were more like Cindy," I said with a sigh. "Cindy's so dependable and organized. At least we know where she is all the time. Kathi's got so much going, I can't keep track of her."

"She's just got a lot of energy, honey." Vern understood and adored our daughter, and I felt, fretfully, he was taking her side against me.

"You can't compare them," he went on. "She is herself. And she'll not only make the cheerleading team, but she'll be head cheerleader. You'll see."

Vern was right. Later that year Kathi was elected head cheerleader for Cleveland High, and we weren't surprised when she was voted the girl with the most school spirit. Whatever were the ingredients that made up enthusiasm, spirit, and excitement, Kathi had them all.

Sixteen! Going on seventeen! Her friends said she was "real cool," and I knew she was popular with her peers. Her eyes, dark and shining under thick lashes, always held a ready smile for strangers as well as friends.

"Kathi, did you make your bed?" I would call as she streaked down the stairs and out the door. It was too late, but I already knew the answer.

"Kathi, why don't you clean your room?" Cindy, usually so even-tempered, would ask shortly.

I'm sure we were all a puzzle to Kathi. She couldn't see what harm her own messy room could do to us. There was so much fun and excitement "out there," so much to do, so many places to go . . . no time to waste. But she would promise to really get busy and clean her room, "as soon as I get back."

Her promises were short-lived!

And the telephone! It became an insistent thing, especially during the dinner hour.

"Kathi," I said finally, after I had gotten up from my dinner three times to answer it, "would you *please* ask your friends not to call between five and six?"

Even Vern, who was long on patience, became agitated with her on occasion.

"Kathi, did you park the car in the driveway like that — right in the middle?"

But our demands and our frustrations were lost on Kathi. We were all so "uptight," and she couldn't understand why. I think she chalked it up to old age and let it go in one ear and out the other.

Friction increased and tension mounted during those teen years, caused partly, I'm afraid, by the constant comparison I made between her and Cindy. Cindy, always the balance, always the one able to adjust, accepting and performing her duties without question, was a mother's dream.

"I forgot; honestly I did." And Kathi's huge dark eyes would be all innocence when I scolded her. "I know I was supposed to be home, but I just forgot." When I needed her, she had just run out the door. When I wanted to use the phone, she was on the upstairs extension. When I had a list of chores for her, she was sleeping. When I wanted her to run an errand, she would take the car and forget to come home for hours.

Kathi had anxiously awaited her sixteenth birthday and the long-anticipated trip to the Department of Motor Vehicles for her driver's test. She had taken six months of driver's training, and now she was *ready*. And she passed

41

the test with flying colors. As we left, she clutched the precious piece of paper in her hand.

"Now keep it in your wallet," I warned her as we drove home. I knew her breezy manner with possessions.

"I will — I will," she assured me, but I noticed that very shortly it was placed carelessly on the dashboard of the car. That's where it stayed, and later that week when Kathi went out driving with Sharon and a few others, a little piece of paper "just flew" out of the open window of the car, to the screams and shrieks of the girls. It took five girls, on hands and knees, scrambling around in an open field for an hour, to retrieve the crumpled license.

And that was not the last time she lost it.

"Do you know how many times I've signed for your license?" I scolded her one day, two years later, when she brought home a form to be signed. "This is the third time you've lost it."

"I know, mom," she said humbly. "This time, I'll keep it in my wallet."

She did; however, the little green wallet was lost soon after that and was mailed back to us after she no longer needed it!

Kathi simply didn't have time to keep things in order, for she was too busy with friends who were constantly calling or coming for her. After she had rushed out of the house, I would go to her room for a brief inspection tour. One look at her disorderly array of clothes, books, and cheerleading gear always left me furious. I couldn't believe that in spite of repeated warnings and scoldings she could leave things in such a mess.

When she was home, there were phone calls constantly, some very late at night. Sometimes friends would come to see her when she should have been in bed. Like Jim, football star at Cleveland and Kathi's "buddy," who threw tiny stones at her bedroom window late at night to get her attention. When we questioned her about leaning out the window to hold midnight conversations, Kathi said, "But, mom, it's Jim, and he wants to talk to me. He has to talk to *someone.*"

Jim was "special." Because he came from a broken home, he aroused all her understanding and sympathy.

When the phone rang late at night, we asked, "Who is that calling so late?"

"It's Glen. He's upset, mom, and wants to talk to somebody." Glen had just lost his sister in an automobile accident, and we found it difficult to forbid his late calls for Kathi's whispered words of comfort.

And, of course, there were always the repeated calls from Felicia. A simmering anger was building up in me toward her because she always seemed to "be there" when I needed Kathi. Their friendship was deepening, and I was troubled by it.

I was determined that Kathi would widen her circle of friends to exclude Felicia.

Kathi and Felicia

8

THE FALL OF 1968 was an important time for our family. Cindy and her fiancé Don were planning their November wedding, and Kathi was a senior — the whirlwind of activities grew to mountainous proportions.

Cindy and I had started planning the wedding in the summer. Every weekend was occupied with a search for just the right bridal gown and an appropriate maid-of-honor dress for Kathi. Finally Cindy settled on an old-fashioned lace dress with high Victorian collar and bell sleeves. And Kathi found hers — a sapphire blue velvet with white lace cuffs.

There was only one objection to the date of Cindy's wedding, and that came from Kathi. It was on the same night as the big football game at Cleveland High!

"But, Kathi," I remonstrated, "this is Cindy's wedding — it's her day."

"Maybe I can leave right after the wedding," she thought aloud.

"Oh, no! Cleveland will do just fine without you for one night."

Two weeks before the wedding we faced another minor crisis with Kathi. She had been selected as one of the candidates for Homecoming Queen, and she begged to wear her maid-of-honor dress for the final selection night. Cindy and

I objected violently; we could imagine Kathi coming home with it all wrinkled and bedraggled with mud. However, she won and wore the lovely blue gown.

"Can you imagine our Kathi as *queen?*" Vern, our boys, and I sat in the bleachers watching the smiling candidates ride around the football field in open convertibles. Felicia was in front of us holding Kathi's photograph on a placard, which read, "Vote for Kathi Johnson. Kathi for Queen." The photo was one of Kathi standing under a tree, the sunlight catching her shining hair, her head tilted with a half-smile on her lips.

"I wish Kathi had worn white like the other girls." I fretted.

"She looks beautiful," Vern said with pride and conviction.

Kathi was elected a princess, quite a change for our tomboy daughter. There was a lump in my throat as I watched her ascend gracefully to the rostrum. Her friend Sharon stood beside her — they had been in school together since junior high and remained close, warm friends.

After the game, Kathi was off to a party with her friends. As they were leaving, I heard a group of excited girls talking. One said, "Wasn't Kathi Johnson beautiful?" I knew she was popular, but I was beginning to find out how much Kathi was really loved by all her friends.

Cindy's wedding day arrived — a cool November day — and the house was in turmoil. Cindy and Kathi hurried to the beauty parlor early in the morning, only to arrive home in tears at what the experts had "done" to their hair. They both brushed the curls out furiously until they had just the style they wanted.

Cindy was radiantly beautiful as she walked down the aisle with her father, and my eyes filled with tears as I saw the look of love on Don's face.

Kathi stood erect and ladylike beside Cindy, stunning in her blue velvet dress. At that moment it was hard for me to envision her enthusiastically leading a cheer at a football game. My girls were beautiful, shining, and happy.

Cindy told me later that tears streamed down Kathi's cheeks throughout the ceremony; her love for her only sister became apparent as she stood next to her, realizing that things would never be quite the same again.

After the reception at the church, we had a small reception at home for close friends and family. In the midst of the festivities, Kathi charged downstairs in her cheerleading outfit. It was the night of the big game, and she still had time to make the last half. While the guests watched, amazed and amused, she kissed Cindy good-by and dashed out the door.

"Typical," I sighed to myself.

I had mixed emotions that night as I thought of losing my oldest daughter, yet I felt that now perhaps Kathi would draw closer to me. I resolved then to make it up to Kathi — all my impatience, all my intolerance; somehow I knew that we would grow to understand and appreciate each other.

Kathi (on top), head cheerleader for Cleveland High

9

FALL WAS IN THE AIR, the football game on television was the center of attraction in our family room, the table was set, and the turkey was ready to be served.

Cindy and Don, radiant in their newlywed happiness, sat to my left. Vern's parents, who had come from Michigan for the wedding, and my mother were across from me, and Kathi and the boys were next to Vern.

He began to pray, "Heavenly Father, thank You for this special day that has such meaning to us as believers in Your Son. Thank You for Jesus Christ and His finished work on Calvary. Thank You for our families, all well and strong and together this day. Thank You for this food so bountifully given. Thank You, Lord, for all Your unmeasured love and grace given to us, Your children."

"What's it like being married?" Kathi, with a mouthful of food, asked Cindy point-blank. "Does it get kind of boring?"

Cindy and Don looked at each other, laughed, and assured her it didn't.

Kathi still couldn't believe Cindy was married. She was sure this wouldn't happen to her for a long time; she had places to go and things to do.

We spent the day as many families do on Thanksgiving: eating, taking pictures, watching football games from faraway snowy states, thankful for the warmth and sunshine that is our Golden State. We looked at proofs of Cindy's wedding pictures, hardly believing that that beautiful night was over.

When Thanksgiving was past and the last bit of turkey had found its way into hungry mouths, we began our preparation for that most exciting season of the year — Christmas. Vern's folks were staying for the holidays and the children were delighted, especially Kathi who adored her grandparents.

As the season approached, the house became more and more festive; everyone was hiding presents — secrecy was in the air.

Kathi took her grandparents Christmas shopping, running from one shopping mall to another, wherever they wanted to go. Grandma tells how Kathi would walk slowly through the stores with her, helping her in and out of the car — quite a feat for the fast-moving Kathi.

We opened our gifts on Christmas Eve, lighting the fireplace in anticipation of that joy-packed evening. There were squeals of delight as everyone opened "just what I wanted." Kathi and Cindy giggled over their usual gift of slippers, which by now had become a tradition.

We talked and reminisced about Grandpa Joe who was having his first Christmas in heaven.

"I wonder what it's like," Kathi said dreamily, "to really see Jesus and all the people in the Bible." She thought a minute, "I hope it doesn't get boring. I wonder what you do all the time."

But all sadness was dispelled as the opened packages mounted and the gaily colored wrapping paper created so much debris that our living room seemed to get smaller by the minute.

In the background the stereo softly played Christmas carols. A buffet lunch was set out on the table, and Vern and I looked at each other with a quiet contentment. This was our twenty-first Christmas as husband and wife. They had all been meaningful and happy ones. Our blessings could never be counted.

Spring came suddenly, and with it, Easter Sunday. That morning I was at the front of the church at the piano, arranging the music that I would play during the service, when I looked up and saw Kathi and her friend Hope directing nine tall husky fellows down the aisle. She had left home early that morning saying that she was picking someone up for church. *But nine boys?*

At dinner we learned that they were the star football players at Cleveland High.

"How did you manage to get them all to church?" Vern asked her.

"I just told them to be ready and I'd pick them up," she said. "I told them it was Easter Sunday and they should be in church."

Vern and I looked at each other in silent amazement. That was Kathi! When she felt something should be done, she did it.

"And what did they think of the message?" Vern asked.

"I don't know what they thought," she said, "but they heard the Gospel message, and that's what I wanted them to hear — about Jesus going to the cross. And best of all, the Resurrection!"

Later in the spring I began to hear of Kathi's plan to leave home and get an apartment with Felicia.

Kathi had often mentioned, ever since childhood, her desire to be a missionary, "to really rough it in the jungles and tell everyone about Jesus." Now all of this was changing — I thought. Because of Felicia, everything would be different. I was afraid of what might happen to my daughter, leaving home so young.

"You're just going to get in with the wrong crowd, two girls living away from home like that," I said bitterly.

"But, mom, Felicia's folks are moving to Texas right after graduation, and she doesn't want to go," Kathi explained.

"It's out of the question! Besides, how can you afford it? You just don't realize the money involved."

"We have jobs waiting for us at Norm's Coffee Shop.

51

We can do it, mom, just give us a chance!" Kathi begged.

"It's not God's will for you to leave home," I said firmly.

"But what if it *is?*" she questioned through her tears.

I couldn't answer that. I was torn inside, and hurt. *It's your pride,* part of me whispered. *What would your friends say? It would ruin your image of a perfect home.*

The full force of their plans for the move to the apartment struck me just a month before Kathi's graduation. I had to go to the hospital for minor surgery, and when I came home, I was still shaky. But Kathi brought up the subject fearlessly and defiantly. She was determined to go.

"Then go!" Tears of anger and hurt pride were streaming down my face. "Take your clothes and leave."

I threw myself on the bed and sobbed. I was taken back to the hospital that night in pain.

I lay in the hospital bed, calling for Kathi and fighting my feelings and pride. I knew that I must let her go — that in releasing her I would be at peace with my second daughter. I prayed and struggled as I lay there thinking of my little girl, now grown-up, and I came to a decision.

When I returned home from the hospital, Kathi was playing the piano. She turned on the bench and faced me. I walked to her, hugged her to me, and began to cry, gently at first.

"Kathi, I'm sorry." I held her face in my hands and looked into those luminous dark eyes that were beginning to spill tears. "Let's try, really try, to understand each other. As soon as you graduate, I'll help you find an apartment, if that's what you really want."

And then the flood of tears broke loose.

Graduation was only a few days away, and Kathi was running faster than ever, upstairs and down, in and out, greatly excited and very happy. Actually much of her attention was focused not upon graduation itself, but upon the all-night party at Disneyland, the annual treat given to high school graduates of the Los Angeles area. Every girl has a beautiful new dress for the occasion, and dates are made far in advance.

"What are you wearing to Disneyland?" I asked Kathi about a week before the big event. Her answer was non-committal. Why bother about something a whole week away? There was so much to do *now*.

On the day of graduation the phone rang in Vern's office.

"Do you have a daughter, Kathi?" a voice asked. It was the May Company department store, asking if she could use our charge account for the purchase of a dress. Vern consented.

At six-thirty that night, a half-hour before she was due to leave for the graduation ceremony and then Disneyland, I was frantically taking up the hem of what already seemed to me to be a micro-mini dress. My fingers were shaking and the usual furor pervaded the atmosphere.

"Why couldn't you have done this sooner?" I scolded.

No answer.

"You're going to be late, Kathi! You drive me to distraction."

But when Kathi put the dress on, my anger vanished. She looked like an angel in the black and white polka dot frock with huge sleeves. Since that day we have called it the "Angel Dress."

As she hurried off, she said, "Felicia and I have dates with Brad and Jon — she with Brad and I with Jon — but we're going to switch."

"You're going to switch?" I repeated, baffled.

"Yeah, we decided Brad likes me better and Jon likes Felicia better, so we're going to switch!" Logical.

"Oh," was all I could think to say as she flew out the door. "Have fun."

She did. She slept all the next day, but when she woke up she recounted the fun of the evening with excitement still dancing in her eyes. The all-night party had been a big success for Kathi.

Kathi at the beach, 1969

10

"WHEN ARE FELICIA'S FOLKS LEAVING?" I asked Kathi soon after graduation.

"In July," she answered quietly. "But she's coming back, mom, and we're going to find an apartment."

I didn't answer her, but I was praying silently, asking for wisdom to understand and to let her go.

"Let her go in love," someone advised, "and she will return in love."

One night in early summer I took Kathi apartment hunting. We drove all over the Valley, talking to apartment managers and giggling together. The door of communication was opening slowly, and I felt a sense of peace which I hadn't known for a long time.

Secretly, I was hoping that she would never find an apartment and that Felicia's folks would insist that she stay in Texas — anything to keep Kathi home.

"What about college?" I asked her.

"I'm going to college; I've already registered at Pierce. I'm going to work at Norm's Coffee Shop this summer. The girls there are making lots of money. Hope and I are going to train in Los Angeles and work in Westwood."

"What about Felicia?" I ventured.

She was quiet for a minute, then said sadly, "She has to go to Texas with her folks."

"Good," I said too quickly, and Kathi bristled.

"You don't understand! Felicia is my best friend. I love her."

"She should be with her parents in Texas. And you should be here."

We were on the verge of another explosion, so I walked away to let the tension subside.

After Felicia left, Kathi was busy with her work in the evenings and trips to the beach during the day. Her little black Volkswagen, which Vern had helped her buy on her eighteenth birthday, in exchange for her working after school at his office, wound its way down the road of Topanga Canyon toward the beach almost every day — packed with friends.

Kathi loved the beach. She would run to the waves and scream with delight as they broke over her. While some of her more sedate friends were basking in the sun on the beach, she was body surfing or running up and down on the sand — her long dark hair plastered down with sea water.

But one hot July day Kathi's little black bug refused to climb the hill, homeward bound. She called a friend, who picked her and her friends up, and left the car at a service station at Malibu.

"I don't know what's wrong with it," she told Vern that night. "It just won't go."

Vern went to the beach and towed the car home. The mechanic at the Volkswagen garage told us that the engine was "through functioning" — totally gone.

Now Kathi was faced with the problem of transportation to her work.

"What in the world are you going to do?" I asked her.

"I'm not going to worry about it," she said.

"But you still owe money on the VW. How can you buy a new one?"

"I will . . . I will." Kathi's usual resolve came to her rescue. But each day the phone would ring at the office and her half-apologetic voice would say, "Mom, what shall I do about getting to work?"

It was then that Kathi began to realize what a family is all about. Vern and I, often at a great inconvenience to ourselves, would leave the car for her so that she could drive to work. She began to see our love and concern and responded to it. By the end of the second week of July, we noticed that something was happening to Kathi. Her attitude was different. She began to care more for her family, and the rebellious, independent spirit seemed to be more under the Lord's control.

But there was still the old problem — Felicia.

Early in July we had taken a short vacation with the boys, visiting Cindy and Don in Garden Grove, Disneyland, and the San Diego Zoo. When we arrived home, there was a letter from Felicia's sister on Kathi's desk.

My heart sank. Sure enough, Felicia had run away from home and was back in California. I called her mother and we talked — both of us in tears. I promised as bravely as I could to look after Felicia.

When Kathi came home that night, I confronted her with, "Have you heard from Felicia?"

She avoided my eyes.

"I know she is back in California. I talked to her mother today. She is worried sick. How could Felicia run away like that?"

Kathi was torn, and I knew it. When Vern came home, we both tried to talk to her.

"Kathi," Vern said, "you don't want to leave home, do you?" She shook her head without looking up.

"It's because you promised Felicia, isn't it?"

I swallowed hard. "How about if Felicia comes to live with us?" Kathi looked up quickly; she couldn't believe her ears.

"We'll fix up your room for the two of you," we told her.

I was sure this would be the answer, and that night Vern and I went to Norm's Coffee Shop for dinner. Kathi greeted us.

"Guess what?" she was dancing with excitement. "I'm not leaving home. Felicia is coming to stay with us." My heart sank, but I promised myself I would be fair and give her a chance.

I spent the next day fixing Kathi's room for two, adding an additional chest of drawers. When they came home, I welcomed Felicia as best I could to our family. Felicia was crestfallen; this was not what she wanted.

It lasted one night, and Felicia again was after Kathi to get an apartment.

The end of July was Vern's birthday, and we drove to my mother's house for a special dinner with the family. When we arrived, we found a beautiful package with a card for "Daddy." It was an expensive shirt from Kathi, who had made the long detour on her way to work to leave the gift for the celebration.

After dinner we went — all twelve of us — to Norm's for dessert. Kathi was delighted when we walked in and gave us special service. We were proud of the tiny, smiling waitress, her dark hair piled high on her head, running around the coffee shop as if on air.

"That smile never leaves her face," my sister-in-law said, nudging me. "Just look at her."

It was true. She smiled at everybody and enjoyed waiting on people. No wonder that her tips were so high! She gave everyone personal, special treatment. I remembered one night when she had come home elated because a customer had given her a $2.00 tip "just for your smile." Now I could see why. Kathi's magnetism constantly drew people to her, for her love for them was open and genuine.

One night, on a previous occasion, I had been irked by her friendliness with three hippie-type boys who were talking to her as they left the restaurant. Kathi smiled, patted them on the back, and told them to be sure and return. She seemed to know them, and I was worried. I cringed at the sight of their long, unruly hair and their careless dress. But none of this bothered Kathi.

"Who were they?" I had asked her later. "I hope you're not too friendly with them."

"Mom," Kathi rebuked me, "how can I reach people if I'm not friendly? We are told to love one another."

Of course she was right, my heart told me. Kathi had learned to love and accept people as they were.

I was to learn later that not only the customers, but also her employers and fellow workers had seen the love of Christ shining through her life. If someone was "low" or "blue," Kathi had ready words of comfort. When a girl at work wanted a day off, it was Kathi she called on to work for her.

"Kathi, it's your day off," I frowned. "You just let people use you."

"It's okay, mom," she'd smile, and go off to fill in at Norm's — endearing herself to another grateful friend.

Now Kathi was serving us the birthday dessert of ice cream piled high with strawberries. My brother was teasing her about the tip he would leave, and she was running back and forth with the coffee pot, her dark eyes sparkling. Once I caught her eye and we both grinned.

That evening marked a turning point in our relationship. After that, each night I would meet her at the door, even though it was close to midnight, to chat and laugh over the happenings of the day — over a cup of coffee we shared a special closeness. She would stack her tip money in small piles and we would count it together.

"I'll soon be able to buy a car," she said.

One night I touched her hand and said, "Kathi, I never really understood you and I'm sorry."

"That's all right, mom, nobody does. But I do. I understand myself."

During Kathi's free time, she and Felicia continued their search for an apartment. Finally they found one close to our home. They moved the middle of August, one day before my birthday.

The evening of the Saturday that Kathi moved out, she

called to say, "Be sure and pick me up for church in the morning. And I'm going to grandma's with you for your birthday dinner."

The next day she was excited as she carried a big package. After dessert, she placed it on the table in front of me. The card said simply, "Love, Kathi." And inside was a three-piece pants outfit, bright red, which fit perfectly.

"It's darling, Kathi."

"And it fits me, too," she giggled. "Now promise you won't take it back. I want you to have it for your vacation."

Our son David, who had gone shopping with her, told us that she had sought out my own special dress shop and my favorite sales person and had paid for the pants suit in quarters — her tips.

Although living away from home, Kathi was actually with us more than she had ever been. Each night she would either call or come over to share her plans with me. And we tried to help her by sharing our car with her; she was visibly moved at our concern for her.

One night as we sat chatting in the den, I mentioned a dream I had had recently. Kathi bolted up in her chair and looked at me intently.

"Was I coming through the door?" she asked.

I was surprised. "Of course not." Her question puzzled me. Then I realized she was referring to some "strange" dreams I had had in the past — dreams where my father and my aunt were walking through a door — dreams I had had just before we received news that they had gone to be with the Lord.

The week after my birthday, Kathi and I made plans to meet for lunch and shop for clothes for our vacation. When she bounced into the office on Thursday, she looked lovely in a white mini dress, her long, dark hair held back with a band. I smiled to see how much she was trying to please me; she knew that it had irritated me in the past when she had dashed into the office with bare feet and flying hair.

"I'm letting my bangs grow out. See?" she said — and

60

this, too, was something I had urged her to do previously. Soon she was walking around the office, greeting the men with, "Hi! I'm Kathi."

In the restaurant she urged me to have anything I wanted; she was paying for it. We had a happy, relaxed time of conversation, and at one point Kathi said, rather timidly,

"You know, mom, sometimes the people in the restaurant ask me why I have such a smile, and I tell them it's because I have Christ in my heart.

"And now I know what I want to do with my life," she continued. "I want to be a missionary."

"That's wonderful, honey." I touched her hand.

As we were shopping, I felt a oneness with Kathi that had always eluded me. Instead of the usual debate over which clothes were right, we were in agreement over everything she bought.

"Which blouse do you like best? The navy blue or the green?"

"I like the green one, honey," I said, after some deliberation. And it was the green one she bought.

When we walked back to the car, I handed her the keys. "Now drive carefully," I repeated the familiar phrase.

"Thanks, mom." Kathi said those two words with more meaning than anything I had ever heard her say, and they echoed in my ears for a long time.

11

"KATHI," I PHONED HER at her apartment, "we are invited to a farewell dinner for the pastor and the Wallis family, and they want you to come, too. It's Friday night; the Wallises are leaving for Brazil on Saturday."

"I can't, mom. I have to work." Kathi was genuinely disappointed.

I was too, for I wanted Kathi to get acquainted with the Wallis brothers, Dave and John, and I felt that they would really enjoy her. Kathi had seen John when she was cheering for the track team meets between Canoga Park High and Cleveland High and briefly at church.

I had even teased her one day after church, "You know who would be a real good boy for you? John Wallis."

Surprisingly, she met this statement with a smile; usually my choices were not hers.

Jim and Ann Wallis were missionaries from our church to Sao Paulo, Brazil. They were also special friends. Now they would be leaving for their third term, and their three older children would remain in the States.

Ethel, almost twenty-one, was finishing her last year at UCLA; Dave, nineteen, was a freshman at Pierce College; and John, seventeen, had just graduated from Canoga Park High, an honor student and track star. Tall, handsome John was dynamic in his love for Christ and, like Kathi, in his positive expressions of his faith. It seemed inevitable that they should meet — but when?

The swim-dinner party was lavish with food and fun; the teenagers swimming in the pool and playing volleyball at the far end of the yard were wholeheartedly enjoying themselves. I was wistful, wishing Kathi were there.

Although it was a wonderful evening, we were sad that our beloved young pastor was leaving the church to go back East. And the Wallises, so dear to our hearts, would be sailing the next day for Sao Paulo.

I thought back to Jim Wallis's message the previous Sunday evening when he had asked the congregation, in a broken voice, to "look after his precious children" while they were gone. How difficult it must have been for them to say good-by to part of their family.

"I wish you could take Kathi with you," I told Jim. "She would make a good little missionary."

As we said our good-bys, I hugged Ann Wallis and she said, "Well, we'll see you in four years."

Something tugged at me and I thought, *No, Ann, it won't be four years at all.*

The next day friends and family met at the pier in San Pedro to wish them well; it would take over thirty days to make the long trip to Brazil.

Ann kissed her children, turned to give her tall son John an extra hug, and then broke down. John patted her shoulder gently. "Don't cry, mom. I'll save my money and come down at Christmas."

Jim and Ann, with their younger sons Bobby and Jim Jr., walked up the long gangplank, waving bravely with set smiles.

Among the group of friends that day were Joe and Veda Quatro with their five children. The Quatro boys, Steve, Jim, and Mike, were special friends of Dave and John. Mike, just seventeen, was planning on a medical missionary career. Strong in his faith, Mike was a real witness at Chatsworth High, a quiet boy with a quick sense of humor. He was active in our Senior High Department at church

64

and, with John and Dave, would meet with Pastor Smith in his office before the Sunday morning service for prayer. Often as I was hurrying to choir practice, I would see the three boys entering the pastor's study with their Bibles in hand. It was an unusual sight; but then, Dave, John, and Mike were unusual boys.

No sooner had the Wallis family set foot in Brazil when they received a letter from Mike:

> Dear Jim Wallis, Sr., father, Ann Wallis, mother, Bobby and Jim Jr., sons:
>
> This letter should arrive in Brazil about the time you get there. The Lord is working fantastically here. Ethel gave devotions at teen-time, and I thought Jesus would appear at any minute. She told about getting and giving, so I gave a little the next day. I talked to a girl at school and she asked me why I wanted to be a missionary. Wow! One other fella asked if I had witnessed to him before. I had. He said it had influenced him to accept Christ. Next I got an assignment to do research on Israel, and I told the class how God said Israel would go back to the land and all about the return of Christ. One girl was so thrilled about the Bible and what I said. Then I got to read from the Bible in class. Last Sunday, Pastor and us guys prayed for the outpouring of the Holy Spirit. Unbelievable — people were pouring down the aisles.

And the letters John sent his parents were filled with news of his busy life and of his love for Christ. John told them of a Missions Camp in Northern California to which the church was sending four young people.

"Mike, Dave, Kathi Johnson, and I are going," he wrote.

My intuition had been right; when John finally met Kathi, he liked what he saw. One Sunday morning I was wondering why she hadn't come down to sit by me, when I saw them sitting together, getting acquainted. Later, after church, John, Mike, and Kathi were grouped together in excited conversation.

65

"Guess what I'm going to do!" she exclaimed when she came home for dinner that Sunday. "I'm going to Missions Camp with John and Dave Wallis and Mike Quatro."

I was stunned. "You are?"

"And I'm going to drive."

"You are?" I repeated dumbly. But I became as excited as Kathi when she talked about it.

"The church is sending four kids, and they asked *me*." Her face was aglow.

Suddenly, "But I promised I'd drive," she remembered dejectedly.

"What car did you plan on driving," Vern asked, half-smiling.

"Well —" she didn't know.

"Don't worry, we'll find you one."

All of us were in high spirits at Kathi's decision to attend the camp. We would do anything to help her. For even though she had moved in with Felicia, Kathi had finally become "our girl."

John Wallis brought a quiet, strong influence into Kathi's quicksilvery life. She became more stable and relaxed, yet her smile was even brighter, more radiant. She was experiencing answers to her lifetime prayer; she was learning to trust Christ completely.

All the tugging and nagging I had thought necessary to bring my daughter into harmony with God's will had not been needed at all. It was the still, small voice of the Holy Spirit that had wooed and won Kathi; she heard His call and responded.

I was ashamed that I had tried for so long to do the Holy Spirit's work. Never again would I be the spokesman for my children's thoughts. I would tenderly guide them and direct them into faith in Christ, but I would let God Himself do the work of convincing and convicting.

I had learned a valuable lesson!

12

"GUESS WHAT?" KATHI ANNOUNCED. "I asked for two weeks off at work and I can have it. I'm going to Lake Shasta with you and then the following week to Missions Camp."

We had made reservations at beautiful Lake Shasta in Northern California for our vacation. Our friends, Roy and Betty Ramsey, ran Holiday Harbor there, and we were going to spend the last week of August at the lake.

"There's only one thing," Kathi was thoughtful. "I have to be back Thursday night. It's the big East-West game and my last night to cheer."

"But, Kathi, we weren't planning on coming back until Sunday. Lake Shasta is twelve hours away."

"Then I'll take a bus back on Wednesday night. I want to go with you and dad. I want to sit under a tree and just study God's Word."

I called the bus station and found it would take quite a bit of maneuvering to get her back home, but Kathi was sure. She was going to the lake with us, and she was going to cheer at the game. John Wallis and all her friends from Cleveland High School would be there. It was going to be a big night!

Friday evening when I began to run a temperature, I knew our vacation would have to be rescheduled for the following week. I was disappointed, as I had looked forward to sharing the week with Kathi.

"I'm so sorry I got sick, honey," I told her. She sat down on the couch with me and bit her lower lip.

"What shall I do with a whole week off," she asked. Suddenly her face brightened. "I know. I'll take the boys camping on the beach."

"Are you sure?" The thought of such an adventure for myself, at any age, would have been unthinkable. But not Kathi!

"Why not?" she bounced up. "We'll leave right after church tomorrow and be back Thursday."

I was apprehensive, but Kathi was sure. She could do it.

"Well, all right then, but I'll keep Danny home. You and Rich and Dave can go, if you promise to call each day at four."

"I will. I will," Kathi promised.

All that Saturday Vern searched frantically for a car for Kathi to drive to camp the following week. Finally he found a red Mustang and made an offer.

"He'll call me if he accepts," Vern told an anxious Kathi when he got home.

He packed our Impala with all the tenting equipment, while Kathi and the boys ran excitedly up and down stairs carrying things — ice chest, boxes of food, suitcases, and flashlights.

Sunday off they went to rough it — my do-anything, dare-anything daughter with her two younger brothers. That afternoon at four the phone rang.

"We're all set up, mom," Kathi said. "Don't worry. There're millions of people here and we're having a blast."

They swam all day, cooked outdoors — with nothing coming out right — and at night by the lantern light, Kathi would read to them from *Living Letters*.

"Now do you guys get that? Do you understand?

You're getting older, and you should know what it means to be a Christian."

The boys would nod. Kathi had always been their pal when they were little, and now she was a little girl again — playing Monopoly with them, giggling when they woke up all huddled together, running on the beach with them. . . . Those were days they would never forget.

When the phone rang on Monday night and the owner of the red Mustang told Vern he would accept his offer, we were as excited as we knew Kathi would be. Vern spent the next day buying new tires, getting insurance, and financing it for her. I could hardly wait for four o'clock to roll around on Tuesday.

"Guess what's in the driveway?"

"Not the Mustang?" I was unprepared for the scream in my ear.

"Yes, all yours."

Needless to say, they didn't stay another day.

That night as Vern, Danny, and I sat down to dinner, in walked three dirty, tired, sun-soaked kids.

"I can't wait to turn that corner," Kathi had told her brothers, "and see that red car. Man, the folks are really cool."

A heavy compliment from a teen-ager!

Kathi ate her chicken, sitting on the edge of her chair. She just had to be off to show her friends her new car, pulling them out of their houses to "see what I got." Playing the stereo tapes as loud as they would go, she found Sharon and Felicia and off they went.

We didn't see her again until Thursday when she dashed home to get her cheerleading gear, scrambling through her closet for her sweater. She pulled on her short red and white cheerleading skirt, grabbed her pompons, and started for the door.

"Just a minute," I called, reaching for my Instamatic. "Stand right there and give me a good cheer. This is your last night as a cheerleader, and I want a good picture of you."

She kicked her leg high into the air, lifted her pompon, gave me a broad smile — I had a picture I shall always cherish!

13

THE MORNING SUN WAS ALREADY hot when I awoke that following Saturday with a headache. We would be packing and making last-minute preparations for our early Sunday morning start to Shasta. Cindy was in town for the weekend, and I had promised her we would shop later in the day. I had to run to my office to finish a few things before my vacation, planning to be home by noon.

The quiet of a Saturday morning office gave me time to reflect on all that had happened in the past months. The change in Kathi had been so lightning quick. I could scarcely believe that all the years of misunderstanding were over. In letting go of her, I had found her; in letting her grow up to make her own decisions, I had gained a daughter worthy of my trust. Though I had so dreaded her moving away from home and in with Felicia, this had actually drawn her closer to her family.

My heart was light and grateful as I put away my typewriter and cleaned off my desk. It would seem so good to be away for a full week — to fully relax. I locked the door and drove home.

When I got there, Cindy was waiting.

"Kathi stopped by earlier and wanted to take me to breakfast, but I told her we'd wait for you. She is coming back, and we'll go to lunch together."

71

Cindy paused a moment, "Mother, have you noticed the change in Kathi?"

I smiled, "Yes, Cindy, I've noticed."

Cindy seemed puzzled. "She's been so sweet to me, and seems to be —" she groped for the right word, "at such peace."

I smiled, happy that Cindy had noticed too. Now, finally, *finally*, the three of us could have a good relationship.

"Thank You, Lord," my heart whispered.

Kathi walked in a few minutes later, sunburned from her days at the beach.

"You bad girl, we get you a car and don't see you for two days," I teased her.

She smiled. "I've been busy getting ready for camp. I have to be at work at four o'clock. Maybe we should take two cars."

I assured her we'd have her back in plenty of time.

For lunch, we found a small chicken place. Kathi, who usually was so bouncy and talkative, was quiet and thoughtful.

We chatted about Camp Hammer. "Do you have a warm coat for cool evenings?" I asked. "Now don't *you* drive, Kathi. Let the boys drive."

She promised she would take along warm clothes and that she would let the boys drive, but her thoughts still seemed far away.

We finished eating and drove on to the department store where the girls would shop while I bought groceries for our trip.

"Good, I'll get to say good-by to Sharon." Kathi clapped her hands. Sharon had been her friend since junior high school days; they were such look-alikes that I always had to look twice when Sharon walked in the door.

When I had finished my shopping, I walked next door to meet the girls. I couldn't find them, so I asked the door-man to page Kathi Johnson.

Finally I found her talking to Sharon, who worked at

the soda fountain, and when the doorman called her name, she grimaced.

"Oh, *mother*," she groaned in embarrassment.

I hugged her. "Just think, now everyone in the store knows that Kathi Johnson is here."

"You'll stop by after work tonight, Kathi?" I asked when we got back to the house. "About midnight?"

"Yes, mom, I want to drop off my tip money so you can put it in the bank for me. I'll say good-by then."

"Now take care of yourself, honey," I called as she got into her car.

"Have fun," Cindy waved.

We stood there, waving and smiling, watching her drive off; we stood on the driveway until the red car turned the corner and was out of sight.

My head still ached. It was so hot, and there was still some packing to do. Suddenly I was depressed and very tired.

When Vern came home, we decided that we would leave earlier than previously planned, so Vern called Kathi at work.

"Yeah, dad?" her voice was bright.

"Kathi, when you come tonight, just leave the money on the table. We've decided to leave at four in the morning and are going to bed early."

He told her to drive carefully and gave her the number where we could be reached at Shasta — "just in case." I was standing beside him, but I didn't reach for the telephone to say good-by. After all, in only a week we would all be home — together again.

Camp Hammer

John and Kathi at camp, day before the accident

14

LAKE SHASTA LAY BEFORE US, blue and sparkling, like a diamond in the sun. We drove along the lake in excited anticipation of our week-long stay at a cabin on the waterfront.

"It's so big," the boys exclaimed. We weren't prepared for the expansiveness nor the beauty that surrounded the mountain lake. It was the Sunday of Labor Day weekend, and we were looking forward to the peace and quiet on Monday night after the holiday crowd would leave.

It was hot, but the air, after the heavy smog in the Los Angeles area, felt fresh and clear. Our three boys were already picturing themselves out on the lake in a boat, fishing reels in hand; Vern was dreaming of a day of water-skiing. I was silent!

Without telling the family, I was experiencing a deep depression. I was so happy about Kathi going to Missions Camp. Cindy and Don were on their vacation. All was well! Then why, on the long twelve-hour trip, did I feel a continual deepening dread?

Lying there in the boat, the sun shining so warmly, the water so cool and inviting, I felt that all should be well with my world. We swam in our own private cove, ate our lunch on the shore, and lay on our backs on the floating rafts looking up into the cloudless, blue skies. What could

be more beautiful than a Northern California lake, surrounded by majestic mountains, and star-filled nights when
we walked to the beach and sat hand in hand looking out
across the water.

For Vern and the boys, each day was better than the
day before. We ate delicious fresh fish; we visited our
friends, Roy and Betty Ramsey, and had lunch with them,
talking over old times; we spent one whole day on water
skis with a high-powered boat. We lived in our bathing
suits and shorts, and when the sun became too hot, we
took refuge in our air-conditioned cabin and played games
with the boys.

But each day I fought the panic I was feeling. *There is
no reason for it,* I told myself, *everything is all right.* The
girls were certainly having a good time. Although it was
our first vacation without them, they were grown-up now
and had their own lives to live. Now the feeling began to
take the shape of some forthcoming dread. I tried to lose
myself in reading the current best sellers I had brought
along.

Once I passed a telephone booth and wondered if I
should call Kathi at Camp Hammer. She would be so busy
and having so much fun — and besides, I had nothing on
which to base my fears. But I found myself counting the
days and then the hours until we would leave for Southern
California and home.

At last it was Friday. Tomorrow we would take one last
swim, pack the car, and head for home. I could hardly
wait, and I didn't know why.

I sat on the bench at the water's edge Friday evening
watching Vern and the boys fishing. It was nearly dusk.
What was so breathtakingly beautiful during the daytime
became eerie at night. Shadows were lengthening around
the neighboring benches. It was turning cool.

I had loved having two girls, and now my house would
be full of boys. Football, baseball, fishing, and camping
would be the topics in our home.

Maybe that's what was wrong! I was just sad to be so far from Cindy and Kathi, even for a week.

After the fish were cleaned and eaten and we had put the boys to bed, Vern and I walked the short block to the coffee shop for dessert. We chatted with the waitress, talking about our children. I spoke of Kathi and said, "It looks as though we'll have a missionary daughter." It sounded incredulous, even to me.

My depression did not lift. I looked at the clock on the restaurant wall; it was 10:30 PM. *I will remember this night as long as I live*, I thought, and then I wondered why.

We walked back to the cabin slowly; suddenly all the pent-up emotion broke loose. I began to sob convulsively, but I had no reason and could not explain why I was crying. Vern held me gently, but the more he tried to comfort me, the harder I cried. Some nameless fear was gripping me. Again I lifted my prayers to my Heavenly Father, always a comfort in time of need, but the prayers seemed to bounce off the wall.

Vern finally fell asleep, and I begged God to be near, to comfort me, for what I did not know. I held the pillow to me, rocking and crying. Finally, as I walked around the tiny cabin, I stopped as though a sudden pain hit me. I looked at my watch; it was exactly 12:30 P.M.

"Oh, Lord," I cried out, "why aren't you near me?" The only answer I had was the sudden pounding of my heart. Something deep within me was hurting; I felt as though part of me was being snuffed out.

I lay back on the bed, and as the tears ran down my cheeks, I turned my thoughts towards Kathi. Tomorrow they would be starting home. I smiled in the dark. I wondered if Jim and Ann Wallis in Brazil knew that Kathi had gone to camp with their boys. I began to write them a letter mentally:

Dear Ann and Jim . . . Isn't it wonderful that God has brought Kathi and John together. I hope you are as happy as I am. . . . I drifted off finally to the blessed relief of sleep.

Four o'clock! A knock at the door in the middle of the night. Something each parent has thought of and perhaps dreaded. For most it never comes. For us it did!

I heard through the grogginess of a deep sleep the voice of Roy Ramsey calling Vern. "Vern, could you come to the office? There's a telephone call for you."

I jumped from bed and the words came tumbling from my lips, "It's Kathi."

Vern left to answer the phone; suddenly, I knew why I had been depressed all week. I was being prepared for this moment. I sat on the edge of the bed, knowing I must get dressed and join Vern in the office, but I had something to do first. I had to talk to the Lord. And then so suddenly and so sweetly His presence was there. His peace came to me so quickly, I can only describe it as overwhelmingly real.

When I walked into the office, I saw the stricken faces of Roy and Betty and Vern in tears.

"Tell me, honey," I begged. "What happened? Who is it?" But, of course, I knew when I heard him saying, "A head-on collision."

"Tell me, tell me," I insisted.

When he hung up the phone and turned to me, he said quietly, "Kathi, Mike, and John have been killed. Dave is in the hospital in Salinas and is not expected to live. It happened about 12:30. Apparently the kids decided to head for home."

Midnight! I saw myself standing in the middle of the cabin looking at my watch and feeling the sudden pounding of my heart. A tiny part of me had been snuffed out at that moment when Kathi lay dying in faraway King City.

Immediately my thoughts were in Brazil with Ann and Jim Wallis. I remembered Jim standing in the pulpit and asking that the people of our church care for their precious children. Now their handsome son John was gone and Dave was critically injured.

"Oh, God," I prayed, "let Dave live."

My thoughts went racing to Canoga Park and to Joe

and Veda Quatro. Their second son, Mike, was such an appealing, dedicated boy. The pain seemed tripled!

And just like that, a well-known, underlined verse in my Bible popped out at me. "Absent from the body, present with the Lord."

"How close they must have been to the Lord," I said aloud. "Just leaving Missions Camp, they were probably bubbling over with happiness."

"I must call Cindy." Vern dialed her apartment in Garden Grove. He said only a few words before they both broke down.

"You know the camp Kathi was going to?" he said. . . . I took the phone and sobbed, "Go home, sweetheart. Be home when we get there."

We called our parents, and then I thought of Felicia — alone in their new apartment — expecting Kathi to arrive that day.

"I must tell Felicia."

"Who's Felicia?" Betty wanted to know.

What could I say? Who is Felicia? *Felicia's my best friend, mom,* I could hear Kathi saying. *I love Felicia.*

Her best friend whom I resented so bitterly. Now I wanted to see her, to ask her forgiveness, to hold her as though it were Kathi herself.

Roy called Pastor Royal Blue and asked him to drive down from Redding before we left. Pastor Blue had been a camp counselor at many junior high camps Kathi had attended. She loved him and so did we. He arrived in a short time and opened the Bible to the Psalms.

Rich, Dave, and Danny stood numbly by us, hardly believing their so alive sister was gone. We held hands and prayed for the grace of God to be our portion; we prayed for His peace, and how sweetly He provided it. We prayed for Dave Wallis, fighting for his life; and we prayed for Ann and Jim that they might be able to come home; we prayed for Joe and Veda.

Dawn was filtering through the windows when we said

our good-bys to the Ramseys and Pastor Blue. Lake Shasta lay behind us, cold and uninviting.

Vern drove in silence, heading for Salinas to identify our daughter. The boys sat quietly in the back, while I leaned my head on the seat and thought of the past few weeks.

I remembered a day not long ago when Kathi had stood in our den and looked at her brothers.

"Yes," she said, nodding, "you have raised good boys. You have a nice family."

A cold chill had passed over me. "Why, Kathi," I said, "what a thing to say. You are part of this family."

She had turned away. What kind of premonitions had Kathi been having the past months. Now I remembered what she had told a friend, "I dreamt I was on my way to a wedding, on the freeway, and I fell asleep and woke up in heaven."

As we rode along in silence, I thought of my baby, my little girl, who had at last grown into a young woman — my daughter whom I had never really understood. I would never see her laughing face again, never hear her bright, "Hi, mom."

"Now I really understand what the finished work of Jesus Christ means." I broke the silence and looked at Vern. "It means the door to heaven is open to all who believe."

The sustaining grace of God was our anchor; we felt His hand every mile of that long, hot journey.

Finally we had to stop and get the boys some breakfast. When the small, dark-haired waitress poured our coffee, I remembered that night at Norm's Coffee Shop when we had celebrated Vern's birthday. Kathi had been walking on air, smiling, chatting, and laughing. I pushed my cup aside and sobbed openly and unashamedly.

But in spite of all the pain, never once did I have to ask "Why?" I was to know the answer before the week was over.

15

WE DROVE UP THE LONG winding road to the hospital in Salinas and stepped into the coolness of the reception room.

The girl at the switchboard turned to greet us.

"Dave Wallis," Vern's voice was husky. "How is Dave Wallis?"

The girl at the switchboard turned to a nurse standing nearby. The nurse shook her head.

"Very bad. You won't be allowed to see him, but there is a number here for you to call. His sister Ethel has arrived."

With shaking fingers I called the number on the telephone pad.

"This is Pastor Wilson's residence," a strange voice said. I asked for Ethel Wallis.

"Oh, Ethel," I began to cry, "I'm so sorry."

Her voice was steady, "You know, the Lord is with us." Ethel, the same age as my Cindy, had already settled the matter in her heart. She had commited Dave to Christ. Her courage undergirded my own. I told her we would be there right away.

Pastor Ralph Wilson opened his heart and home to our families so graciously that day after the camp director had phoned him about the accident.

We drove to the Wilson residence and straight into the concern and love of fellow believers. Joe Quatro stood there — grief-stricken; Ethel was waiting to put in a shortwave call to her parents in Brazil. Jim Montgomery, chairman of our deacon board and a long-time friend, stood there with Joe.

Already the Saturday morning paper had headlined: "Three die in Greenfield crash."

I read the news report and could hardly believe that was my Kathi they were writing about.

We stood there together in the dining room of the Wilson home, each giving strength to the other, and each receiving strength from the Lord.

When we called the hospital again, Dave had been taken in for emergency surgery.

"Dave must live," I said to Ethel.

"He will," Ethel smiled. "I know he will."

At last it was three o'clock and the shortwave call could go through. Ethel had promised her father she would be calling him that day to wish him a happy birthday. Instead, she must tell him of John's death and Dave's injuries.

The radio message was blurred. Ethel had to shout to be heard. Each word was like a fresh stab of pain to me.

"John killed," she said loudly and clearly, "Dave injured. Make arrangements to come home."

When she finished, she seemed drained of all strength.

"They will try to get permission to leave the country immediately," she said.

Heavy, heavy hangs over my heart. . . . I looked at Joe who was deep in his own thoughts. But all the time I was thinking of the child of my own heart, Kathi. I kept hearing her voice the day I handed her my car keys.

"Thanks, mom," it was ringing over and over in my ears.

"Honey," Vern told me, "I'll drive home with the boys. I want you to fly home with Joe and Jim."

I readily agreed.

"Do you realize," I leaned over to talk to Joe in the plane, "that we all had five children?"

Joe nodded, "I thought of that. And it was our second sons and your second daughter who were taken."

We were silent the rest of the short flight.

My thoughts began to center on one plea. *If only there were a letter from Kathi at home, just a short note telling us about camp. If only . . . if only. . . .* It repeated itself like a broken record in my head. *If only a short note — if only a letter . . . a letter . . . a letter. . . .*

At last we landed at Los Angeles International Airport, and I phoned my mother. She had been waiting for my call.

"I'll meet you at your house." I knew she had been crying.

Jim drove me home, and standing on the driveway — just waiting — was Cindy. We walked into a wordless embrace. There were no words that could express our grief. We had lost Kathi just when we had found her. Cindy understood that only too well.

I walked into the house and sat heavily on the sofa. Cindy turned on a light. Our eyes were swollen; sorrow lay out in the open to be shared. We had both loved Kathi and neither of us had understood her.

I voiced my thoughts then. "If only . . . if only there had been a short note — a letter — from Kathi." I looked around the house as though I expected to find one.

"Well, mom," Cindy sat forward, "I went to see Felicia this afternoon to tell her, and she *did* get a letter from Kathi. I thought you might not want to see it just yet." She opened her purse.

I reached for the two pages Cindy was holding.

"Oh, yes, yes, I do."

I closed my eyes a second before I began to read the familiar handwriting. Felicia had received the letter Friday. Kathi must have written it Wednesday, just three days before the accident.

It was written on the back of some notes, half-written, half-printed, as though she had so much to say and had to say it all right then — no time to waste.

I opened the letter and began to read, and the tears sprang to my eyes and rolled down my cheeks.

Felicia,

This is the first chance I've gotten to write. I've been so busy studying God's Word. This place is the greatest. I have really great times with my brothers and sisters in Christ. I'm learning so much, and yet I know nothing. Felicia, I wish you were here right now. Christ is the only answer and no matter how much Jon, Sharon, Brad, or you think this makes no sense, man, it is the greatest. I've really missed out on a lot because I'm living as the world lives. Oh, if only everyone had my Jesus. I just can't believe how much there is to know and learn. The Christian life is the only life. I don't mean the hypocritical life such as I was living, but being close to the Holy Spirit, trusting him.

Felicia, I'm not gonna fool around with you anymore. You need Jesus. I don't mean as you have him now. You need to walk and talk with him everyday. As your best friend it's my responsibility to see you are not lost. Believe me I know this world has nothing to offer. You may think Jim is the only answer, but he didn't die for your sins. I can't stress enough your need for God. Do you realize what we could achieve together. When you really have Christ in your life as your Master, I guarantee you change. I have failed as a Christian, but believe me, for every person I've failed, three more will learn to trust in Jesus. I know the first thing you'll say is "There she goes again with her religion." I'll tell you something. I don't care what anyone thinks, because everyone needs Jesus. Take time to pray, talk to God, ask him his perfect plan for your life. He has one for everyone, but it's up to you to find out what it is.

Read the Bible. You'll never believe how great it is. Even I can't comprehend its greatness. I can't ever wait until I can read it more. *There's no time to waste* because God is going to judge us and we have to give an account. What have we done for Christ. There are a lot of things we have to discuss when I get home. I'm so excited to tell you. Please don't ignore this. Felicia, pray to God. Ask him to come into your life. Don't be selfish like me, and don't say I won't give in because materialistic things of the world will all be past, but what you do for Christ will last. And you know why you never grew in Christ after you walked up the aisle. Because everyday you must read God's Word and pray. Christ is the answer, and I thank God every time I pray up here for giving me his Son and eternal life.

Felicia, I'm praying for you along with my brothers and sisters up here. I hope that soon you will be my sister too. It's going to be hard for me to go back to the apartment because the Bible says we need Christian fellowship and it's hard for me there. We need to have a heart to heart talk, and I really want to listen to what you have to say. Felicia, I'm out for the world, and if I can't even make my best friend see this way, then I see how difficult the job is. Be good and when I get home we've got a lot of talking to do, I hope.

In Christ's love I write this,

Kathi

John

16

"WHERE'S FELICIA?" I asked Cindy.

"She's coming over later, mom." Cindy then told me how she had gone to the apartment to break the news to Felicia.

"I decided," Cindy said, "I would tell her very calmly, but I didn't. I cried all the time I was telling her.

"Felicia sat as still as stone. Finally she reached for this letter which was lying on the coffee table.

"'At least we know she is with God,' were her words. The moment she said that she began sobbing. I read Kathi's letter and asked her if I could show it to you. She said yes.

"'I guess your mom won't want to see me,' she said softly, but I said, 'Yes, she will.' I knew you would, mom."

And I did. For now I could love Felicia completely and truly, just as Kathi had wanted me to. She had been the closest friend to my daughter and I wanted to see her.

My mother and my brother and his family arrived . . . the phone was ringing . . . the doorbell was ringing . . . friends called to assure us of their love and prayers. And I was anxious for Vern and the boys to arrive from Salinas.

My mother told me how Kathi had come to see her recently. She had been surprised, for it was the first time Kathi had ever visited her grandmother alone.

"I had the day off, grandma," she had said, "and I just thought I'd come and visit you."

They talked together of Kathi's decision to go to Missions Camp the following week.

"I'm so excited," she had said. "I can hardly wait."

When she kissed Kathi good-by at the door, that was the last time my mother ever saw her "sweet Kathi." What had made her take the long detour from Westwood to Pacific Palisades, just to "visit" her grandma?

We learned also that Kathi had made a special trip to Hope's home the day before she left for camp.

"Hope," Kathi had said, "we haven't been as good friends lately, and I'm sorry. I've been praying and praying for God's will to be done in my life, and He has answered. I didn't even ask to go to camp, they asked me."

That was Kathi's good-by to her friend Hope.

And the urgency of the letter that she wrote to Felicia was found in a similar letter to her friend Brad in the Navy.

Kathi's letter to Felicia was a balm in an open wound. I carried it with me and showed it to my family and friends as they arrived.

"It's almost as though she *knew*," some would say. Or, "It's inspired of the Lord."

I went to the door to answer a persistent ring at nine o'clock and there was Kathi's old friend Tom.

"Hi," he was smiling. "Kathi doesn't live here any more, does she?"

I opened the door and asked him to come in the house.

"Tom," I said as gently as I could, "haven't you heard? Kathi was in an accident. She was killed."

I thought Tom was going to faint; he turned white and sat down.

"Read this letter she wrote Felicia three days ago, Tom," and I handed him the cherished paper. He sat down and read it; when he handed it back to me, his eyes were wet.

"What a girl! Telling what she believed loud and clear, right to the end."

I had to smile a moment remembering Kathi and Tom's heated discussions over religious doctrine.

"She's with the Lord, Tom," I assured him, and he nodded.

Around midnight when things had subsided, Vern arrived home with the boys. He enfolded me in his arms to comfort me and was surprised at the peace that had come to me.

"Look, honey." I showed him Kathi's letter.

"I'm out for the world," he repeated. "Only Kathi would say a thing like that." His voice was choked with emotion. "And you know what? She *will* reach the world with this testimony of her faith. Who could resist such an appeal?"

We prayed! We thanked our Heavenly Father for taking our daughter straight home to be with Himself.

"That where I am there ye may be also," Jesus said.

What a comfort!

"Honey," Vern reached for my hand, "she's home free."

Dave

17

SUNDAY MORNING THE DOORBELL RANG; it was Felicia and her mother. When Felicia had phoned her mother in Texas, all she could say was, "Mother, Kathi's dead." Her mother had flown immediately to be with her, and here, for the first time, I met her.

"Felicia, forgive me," I said as I embraced her and began to cry. "I was envious, I suppose, because you and Kathi were so close." I sobbed out all the emotions I had carried inside so long.

The three of us spent most of that day getting to know each other. I could feel Kathi's presence, warm and real, so happy that at last I had accepted and loved her best friend. Perhaps many misunderstandings could have been avoided if we had all met and talked together two years ago.

"Kathi never let me down, not once," Felicia told me. "She promised me if I made it back to California, she'd live with me, at least through the summer. And she kept her word, even though she knew it was hurting you."

Our house was filled with family and friends — Kathi's friends flocked to the door . . . food . . . flowers . . . telephone calls from distant states . . . and always, those words of blessed comfort, "We sorrow not as others who have no hope."

How can one have peace at a time like this, but peace it was — spreading through me, perfect and pure, the peace that passes all understanding — the peace of God.

In faraway Brazil, Jim and Ann Wallis were frantically trying to get permission to leave the country. It couldn't have been at a worse time. All permission had been temporarily postponed due to political upheavals in the government. It looked as though it would be impossible.

Friends all over the United States formed a chain of prayer that God would work miracles to let them come home.

On Tuesday the suspense was great. Dave was still on the critical list, and we had heard no word from Brazil. A few men from our church got together and theorized, "If you wanted to talk to someone in Brazil, what would you do?"

"You would pick up the phone and ask the operator if you could place a call to Brazil," one man said.

"That's what we'll do."

The call went through immediately, and they learned that the Wallises were already in flight on their way home to the States and would arrive in Salinas on Wednesday to see Dave.

We learned later that it had been a miracle from the hand of the Lord to open the heart of a high official of the Brazilian government to allow them to leave at such an inopportune time.

Vern and I knew that, along with Joe and Veda Quatro, we would have to make arrangements for the funeral to be held Thursday.

As we started out the door to meet Joe at the funeral home, I turned to look at Kathi's graduation picture. A casket for her? My vibrant, dancing "that girl"? I held tightly to Vern's hand, gathering strength for the task ahead of me.

When we met Joe at the funeral home, he told us all the details of the accident. The car had somehow gone over the median and into the path of oncoming traffic. How it happened no one knew.

I was picturing the little red Mustang traveling along the curved highway, four laughing teen-agers, talking, munching on candy bars, so happy from their week at camp. Did they see it coming? Was it too sudden for them to realize they were going to have a head-on collision?

However it happened, *why* it happened was not for us to know. And now we had to choose a final resting place for our three children. Our hearts were deeply touched when dear friends graciously offered three graves next to each other in beautiful Oakwood Memorial Park in Chatsworth.

That night when we were home, Vern handed me the tiny blue birthstone Kathi had been wearing at the time of the accident. I held it tenderly. Kathi had loved it so much and had worn it always. I thought lovingly of John, who was in the service now, and remembered the night he had so proudly given Kathi this little ring.

God had again done abundantly above all I could ask or think. I had Kathi's letter, her final testimony to her love for Jesus Christ, and I had this little ring, a tribute to her abiding friendships. I didn't know it then, but I was to have more, so much more.

Mike

FRANK
MORTON

18

"HONEY," VERN TOLD ME, "I think you ought to remember Kathi as she was. I don't think you want to see her as she is now."

He had gone in ahead of me at the funeral home and was quite shaken when he came out. But I knew deep in my heart that I had to see the body Kathi left behind. I knew it would be final for me then.

I walked into the room slowly and looked down at my second daughter. Her dark hair had been brushed and lay loosely about her face. Her bangs had been cut into a wisp on her forehead. The laughing dark eyes were closed. Kathi was gone.

While I stood there, Vern gently put his arm around me, and we both sensed the presence of God. His glory filled the room. It was so real in an unexplainable way. Instead of breaking down as I thought I might, my heart felt lighter, for I knew that this wasn't our Kathi. She was alive right now, more alive than ever, and in a way we could never realize this side of heaven.

Cindy came up beside me, and then Felicia, my mother, my brother, and our boys. Felicia tenderly laid a lovely bouquet of flowers in Kathi's hands. As I watched Felicia's face, the tears did come to my eyes. She had loved and known Kathi so well, perhaps better than any of us. Kathi's last thoughts and prayers had been for Felicia. "It's my responsibility to see that you're not lost," she had written.

When the others turned to leave, I touched Kathi's hand and whispered, "Good-night, honey, I'll see you in the morning." That had always been a part of our good-nights when the children were small. At the door I would turn to say, "Good-night, honey, I'll see you in the morning."

This night would be a little longer, perhaps, but the morning *would* come when I would see my beloved child once more.

Felicia walked to the car with us, deep in thought.

"Do you think I could talk to Pastor Smith tonight?" she asked.

Ivan Smith, our former pastor, had just arrived from the East because we had asked him to officiate at the funeral. We drove Felicia to the home where he was staying, and he took her aside.

"I want to be a Christian," she told him, "just like Kathi."

When Felicia walked back into the room where we were waiting, her face was aglow.

I hugged her; my heart was too full to speak.

Kathi's prayers were answered. Felicia had made a commitment to Jesus Christ and opened her heart and life to Him.

I remembered that day in August when we were having lunch and Kathi had said, "Now I know what I want to do with my life. I want to be a missionary."

Had she lived to an old age, Kathi might never have been able to reach Felicia as she had in death. And had she gone to the mission field as she planned, Kathi might never have reached the thousands who would soon hear the truth of the Gospel because of her death.

How true are the words of the Apostle Paul: "And we *know* that all things work together for good to them that love God."

19

JIM AND ANN WALLIS and their two boys arrived from Salinas bringing Dave home by air ambulance. He was to go into UCLA Medical Hospital for extensive plastic surgery the following week.

We welcomed them into our home, along with Joe and Veda, Pastor Smith, and Roy McKuen, president of World Opportunities, Inc., long-time friend of the Wallis family. Though full of grief, our hearts were completely surrendered to the fact that this was God's will for us. We talked of our children; the Quatros told of Sue and Alissa, friends of Mike, who had received Christ in their home that day; Jim and Ann told of John's friends who were expressing faith in Jesus Christ.

All of us wanted the funeral service the following day to be one of victory — tragedy turned into triumph. We formed a circle and held hands, each of us praying and asking the Lord to bring glory to His name through our children's Homegoing.

We cried together; we prayed again!

What strength God gave us that day — what perfect peace.

When I went to bed that night, I asked God to give me grace and strength for the next day. I wanted the whole world to know that His grace was sufficient to meet every need, even the burying of a daughter.

The long, black limousine came for our family, and we drove to Van Nuys Baptist Church where the service was to be held. It was mid-morning and already warm for an early September day. The vast parking lot was filling with cars.

Inside the beautiful sanctuary, the pipe organ filled the church with glorious sounds. Our family sat in the pew behind the Wallis family, and the Quatros were behind us.

Flowers filled the front where the three closed coffins lay. Over them was a huge cross of flowers sent by the Conservative Baptist Missions Camp where our children had spent the last week of their lives.

And everywhere — teen-agers! I had asked Kathi's friends from school to be her pallbearers — Tom, Jim, Glen, and Jon. I remembered last Easter Sunday when she had brought them all to church.

"I wanted them to hear the Gospel," her words echoed, "about the death of Christ and especially the Resurrection."

Jim was weeping openly. Kathi had been his pal; they had confided their secret wishes and dreams to each other. Glen, who had recently lost his sister in an automobile accident and who had made those midnight telephone calls so that Kathi could "comfort him." Tom — how he and Kathi had laughed and teased each other, often ending in verbal hassles over church doctrine. And Jon, the one to whom Kathi had recently said, "One of us in this crowd is going to be killed in an auto accident."

When I saw Felicia enter, my heart warmed remembering her decision to follow Christ. And just yesterday Felicia's mother had told Pastor Smith, "I've been away from the Lord for many years, but I'm coming back today."

And then I thought of the little card that had accompanied a lovely floral piece that had arrived that morning. "Thank you, Kathi — Bev," was all it had said. Who was Bev?

The sound of a familiar strain from the piano brought me back to reality. It was the Young People's Choir singing

98

a song Kathi had loved to play and sing — "The Father Loves You." It brought Kathi sharply into focus and I remembered the many times she had called her friends to the piano to listen to "this cool song. . . ."

Roy McKuen read the twenty-third Psalm and the words of Jesus in John 14:

> Let not your heart be troubled: ye believe in God, believe also in me. In my Father's house are many mansions. . . . I go to prepare a place for you. . . . that where I am, there ye may be also.

Words I had read and heard all my life now took on new meaning.

Pastor Smith, visibly shaken, began speaking to the crowd of nearly two thousand people.

"I wondered what Scripture I should use at a time like this, and the verse that Mike's dad showed me underlined in his Bible characterizes the lives of these three young people.

> According to my earnest expectation and my hope, that in nothing I shall be ashamed, but that with all boldness, as always, so now also Christ shall be magnified in my body, whether it be by life or by death. For to me to live is Christ, and *to die is gain.*

"These are the same words quoted by Mike at Camp Hammer the closing night of camp, when he stood to his feet and gave his testimony that Christ should be glorified in his body, whether by life or by death. Christ chose to be glorified by Mike's death. . . .

"I asked the Wallis family what John wanted to do with his life. They told me that just before they returned to the mission field, John had said that he 'wanted to preach like Billy Graham and win people to Christ'. . . ."

Pastor Smith then read Kathi's letter to Felicia.

"Kathi must have had a premonition that she was going to be ushered into the presence of the Lord," he continued.

"I believe she wrote this letter as though it was the last thing she might ever do. . . .

"It was the desire of these young people that Christ be glorified in their lives. Already a number of their friends have come to know Christ as Savior. I mean in a personal way, the way Kathi was talking about, not just becoming a member of the church, but knowing the living Christ in a real way.

"If we were to ask Kathi, Mike, and John to say something here today, I know what they'd say. 'We want you to know our Jesus.' And they would tell you heaven is the 'greatest.' That's exactly how they'd express it. For them it was gain to die. You may ask what possible gain could come from their deaths, but I'll tell you — to be absent from the body is to be present with the Lord. We weep and sorrow, but not as others who have no hope, because we know that Kathi, Mike, and John are with Christ. . . .

"If these three were to speak today, they would say, 'I had the most, the greatest — life in Christ. Christ is the greatest. Serve Him now. You can only count on today. There's no time to waste.'"

When he had finished, Roy McKuen asked the audience to stand and sing "When We All Get to Heaven." It was a hymn of glorious anticipation. And as the hundreds and hundreds of people filed past the three closed caskets, the organist played Handel's "Hallelujah Chorus."

There were many poignant moments . . . little Bobby Wallis tugging at the coat of the undertaker and whispering, "Sir, which one is my brother?"

Kathi's grave was between John's and Mike's — as in life, so in death, surrounded by her friends.

20

DEAR MRS. JOHNSON,

I know that you have heard from many of us at Missions Camp. I, too, want to express my sympathy for your loss. How wonderful, though, that we can rejoice in the ways the Lord uses and magnifies the death of His children.

I mainly wanted to write to let you know how highly Kathi spoke of you and Mr. Johnson, and how deep her love was for you. On the first night of camp, Kathi told me that she was living in an apartment with Felicia. Knowing that my parents would put up a bit of a fuss if I moved out, I asked her how you, her parents, had reacted. With obvious pride, she spoke of your concern for her in leaving, but said that you had respected her decision and allowed her to move. She also spoke of how wonderful you were in other ways.

Once, when we spoke of raising our own families, Kathi said how glad she was of the way she had been raised. She felt that she had been guided, instructed, and raised with the greatest love and Christian commitment on your part. She also spoke of her love for her brothers and how she had enjoyed taking them camping the week before.

Kathi spoke of her parents often, and it was always

with the deepest respect and love. She was a beautiful girl, and I'm sure you are proud to be her parents. I pray that this letter will be of comfort to you.

I have never met the writer of that beautiful letter, but it was a balm to me in those days after the funeral — along with many other cards and letters telling of Kathi's faith in Christ, of her beauty in helping others, and always everyone spoke of her genuine love for the Lord and of her constant smile.

We were having dinner one night with friends, only a week after the funeral, when a long-distance telephone call came through for me from Seattle, Washington.

It was Kathi's roommate, Valerie, from Camp Hammer. She wanted to tell me of Kathi's last days, of her joy in surrendering her life to God.

"We went to a service together on Thursday night," she told me, "and the missionary spoke on death. Walking back to our cabin, I said to Kathi, 'You know, Kathi, I would be willing to die if my father would come to know Christ.' Kathi stopped suddenly, as though a new idea had hit her. I could see the thoughts whirling around in her head. Then she said, so softly, 'Yes, I, too, would be willing to die if Felicia and my friends would come to know my Savior.'

"That night Kathi had a nightmare and awoke screaming. 'It was so dark, and I couldn't find the door. I'm so afraid something is going to happen.'

"In the morning Kathi told Dave, Mike, and John about her dream. They sat under a tree, and Dave opened the Bible to Psalm 27: 'The Lord is my light and my salvation; whom shall I fear? the Lord is the strength of my life; of whom shall I be afraid?' Then they prayed, each of them praying that God would use their lives, all of their lives, for His glory, whether by life or death.

"When Kathi walked back into our cabin, her face was radiant. 'Now I've given my *whole life* to Jesus,' she said."

When I finished talking to Valerie, I could only breathe another prayer of thanks to our wonderful Lord.

"It was no accident," I said as I took my place at the table. "God took those kids. He just reached down and took them."

Vern and I drove to the UCLA hospital the following day to see Dave. He was scheduled for plastic surgery soon. When we walked into the room, I was unprepared for what I saw. His face was swollen beyond recognition, his arm in a cast.

He started to rise from his bed. "Mrs. Johnson," he spoke through clenched jaws, "I want to kiss you." I bent down to brush my lips across Dave's face and my tears fell on his cheek.

Dave would have many weeks of wired jaws, more plastic surgery, and much pain, but he grew ten feet tall in the following months. The peace of God was his portion; Dave had committed himself to the Lord.

"I'll have to take up where they left off. We just don't realize how sovereign God really is. It's not, why has God taken them, but *why has He left me.*"

The circle began to widen, ever so slowly, but surely. One Saturday I heard a knock on the door and there stood lovely, blonde Debby, one of Kathi's friends whom I knew only slightly.

"You know what I just did?" she sobbed. "I went to the cemetery, sat down on Kathi's grave, and gave my heart to Jesus."

Between her sobs, I learned that Kathi had been especially kind to Debby in high school. I grew to know and love this girl in the following weeks as she came to our church and our home often. But my heart was deeply touched when some months later she sent me her graduation picture with this note:

"I want to thank you for everything you've done for me. . . . Please help me discover things which I have long neglected. And Christ seems for *now.*"

Then there were Sharon and Hope, both expressing faith in Christ.

But I was soon to hear a story that settled any doubts that God had chosen Kathi, Mike, and John to fulfill a special mission in life. For I was to meet Bev and hear her remarkable story!

21

ON MONDAY NIGHT, two weeks after the accident, Bev finally came to our door. I greeted the glowing girl with a hug.

"Kathi was so great," she began after we sat down together over tea and cookies. "I guess you want to know why I signed my card, 'Thank you, Kathi.'"

"I do, I do."

Bev flipped her long hair back in typical teen-age fashion.

"I was at the beach with some kids from my club when we heard about the accident. Most of the girls were in swimming, but a few of us were just sitting around talking, when all of a sudden we heard a scream and one of the girls came running down the hill crying, 'Kathi Johnson has been killed.'

"We were all stunned. Not Kathi, I thought. Kathi had been so alive and always so excited about everything. My friend Mary and I had just been talking about God and how we just couldn't believe there could be a God, you know, with all the bad stuff going on in the world. And now this news about Kathi. I just couldn't believe God would let her die."

We both wiped the tears from our eyes as Bev continued.

"After awhile the other girls went away, and Mary and

I were sitting there crying and talking about Kathi when all of a sudden two girls walked up to us. They said, 'Could we share something with you?' We nodded.

"Then they told us about the four spiritual laws and how God loves us and has a plan for our lives.

"We listened to everything they said, especially because of the news we had just heard about Kathi. When they asked us if there was any reason why we couldn't let Christ into our hearts, we knew there wasn't. Mary and I both bowed our heads and put God on the throne of our hearts instead of ourselves.

"Now there seemed a reason to be living. Everything that had puzzled me before fell into place.

"If it hadn't been for Kathi's death and the faith I knew she had placed in Christ, I might never have known the Lord. That's why I said, 'Thank you, Kathi.'"

Bev's radiance was real, her joy unmistakable. I thought of that gem of a verse in Corinthians, "If any man be in Christ, he is a new creature: old things are passed away; behold, all things are become new."

In the months to come I saw the "new" things in Bev's life: her new faith, her new goals, her new desires. I couldn't help but look at Kathi's smiling picture and repeat, "Thank you, Kathi."

One Sunday in church Bev handed me a small folded piece of paper. On it she had written these words:

> I had a friend,
> And I didn't know it,
> So caught up was I in my own world.
> I ignored an outstretched hand full of warmth.
> My friend is gone, but I feel the warmth.
> My friend left me LIFE.

As we shared the decisions of Kathi's friends with the Wallises and the Quatros, they had much to share about friends of Mike and John. They, too, had left a tremendous impact on their friends. It was John's aunt, Ethel Emily Wallis, author and missionary, who conceived the idea of printing a small booklet in memory of our three children. Under her capable hands, we watched the booklet grow into a highly polished, eight-page brochure called "The Winning Team."

On the cover was a picture of John Wallis breaking the tape for Canoga Park High's track team. Inside, pictures of Kathi, Mike, John, and Dave graced the colorful pages, with their testimonies, snapshots taken at Camp Hammer, a newspaper clipping about the accident, and an excerpt of the funeral message.

The last paragraph read: "If you would like to know more about the God of Kathi, Mike, and John, write to Dave Wallis."

It was distributed to each student at the three high schools and began making its way into homes all over the San Fernando Valley and even into faraway states.

As thrilling as the response to the booklet was the Sunday morning service at which it was dedicated. The church was filled to capacity; many school friends of the four were there. And at one point, Felicia gave her first testimony for Jesus Christ.

"I know many of you think it was Kathi's letter that brought me to Christ, but it wasn't. It was her *life*. I knew her and lived with her, and I knew she had something I didn't have — something I wanted. Now I know it was Jesus Christ. And I don't have to be afraid or lonely anymore. I have Christ with me *always*. I only want God's will for my life."

It was a shining moment! But only a foretaste of the real glory when we stand before the Lord and really *know* the countless souls brought to heaven because of Kathi, Mike, John, and Dave. . . .

"Remember, things don't just happen to those who love God," I could hear my dad saying. "They are planned."

"We prayed before we left camp," Dave told us. "We all prayed that the hand of God would be on our car."

And their prayers were answered — not exactly the way they might have expected, but answered — in God's perfect timing. God had heard their dedication in promising Him *all* and had taken them at their word.

As letters began coming in to Dave, I thought of the line in Kathi's letter to Felicia. "For every one I've failed, three more will come to trust in Jesus."

Dave, so miraculously recovered, began answering the letters, sharing his faith with the many who asked for help. And Dave shared some of the letters with me, all written with the same plea — from teen-agers, from grandmothers, from servicemen, and even from a high school coach — "Help me find God!"

> Dear Dave,
> I read the small story of you and the other three of your Winning Team and I really felt a touch of our Lord's goodness. I suppose you have many people ask you how you can be glad when your friends and your very own brother were killed, but they don't understand that they have already reached the home we want to have when we die. I only came to Christ a few weeks ago, but I am so glad I did. How can I tell my friends about Christ? Should I write a letter similar to what Kathi wrote to her friend Felicia and what she told her? I am wondering about this. Please help me.

> Dear Dave,
> I read the pamphlet on "A Winning Team" and was very impressed by it. I would very much like to know about the God of Kathi, Mike, and John. So as the pamphlet stated to do, I am writing to you for this information. I hope that through you I can find the God of Kathi, Mike, and John. My sincerest thanks.

> Dear Dave,
> I have read the magazine called "A Winning Team." I am of another faith but would like to know how others feel about God. I would like to know more about the God of Kathi, Mike, and John. I am a captain of a cross-country team.

Letters upon letters, all answered by Dave, who had promised to "take their place."

22

I EXPERIENCED A SHARP THRILL when I looked around at the people gathered in our living room. Some were Kathi's friends, some had never met her, but all had heard of the accident, read "The Winning Team," and wanted to begin a Bible study class.

I thought of Felicia who had gone back to Texas with her mother.

"I want to help her now," Felicia said — Felicia, the rebellious girl who had run away from home. "I want to tell my brothers and sisters about Jesus."

She had given me a card before she left, and when I opened it and read the words there, I longed for Kathi to know, too.

Dear Mrs. Johnson,

One of the things Kathi wanted most was that I become her sister in Christ. Now that is a reality. And being her sister makes me your daughter. I love you.

I would always love and pray for Felicia.

One night Steve came to our Bible study, and I knew from the moment I met him that God had great things planned for him. Steve endeared himself to Vern and me immediately. His desire to know more about God was all-consuming; his prayers were simple, direct, and challenging to our own hearts.

Steve, who had come from a broken home, would soon move in with Dave Wallis, who was to become a great influence in his life. The night Steve confided to Vern and me that he wanted to be a minister was a high point for us. Later Steve brought his friend Janie to the group, and after listening and studying, she, too, came to know Christ personally.

As the members of the group opened up to each other, we were all drawn closer to one another and to Christ. Our last Bible class met just before the Christmas season, and as each went his or her own way, I was thankful for the time of sharing and growing we had had. In losing Kathi, I had gained numerous sons and daughters in Christ.

The day before Christmas I went alone to Oakwood Memorial Park and laid flowers on the three graves. The markers were new, and I fought back the tears as I read the verses each family had chosen.

On Mike's, his favorite: "For to me to live is Christ, and to die is gain."

John's marker read: "I have fought a good fight, I have finished my course, I have kept the faith."

And for Kathi's we had chosen: "To be with Christ, which is far better."

Oh, Kathi, I thought, *if only I had really taken the time to know and understand you.* As I turned to go back to the car, that verse about entertaining "angels unaware" ran through my mind, and these words came to me:

> I had an angel and didn't know it;
> She hurried through life in a breathless sort of way,
> She touched this one and that one in her short life span,
> Like a candle burning wildly and then flickering out too
>   soon,
> For one brief, shining hour she warmed so many with that
>   glow.

110

We sat around the tree on Christmas Eve and opened gifts, and for the first time, Cindy had to open her traditional pair of slippers alone. But instead of the terrible longing for Kathi which I had anticipated, my heart was filled with a special kind of joy — the joy that only Christ can bring! For sharing our first Christmas without her were Hope, Debby, Bev, and Kathi's old boyfriend John — and a warm long distance phone call from Felicia.

They missed her, too, for they had found a deeper meaning to life because of knowing her. And without saying it, we all felt her presence.

Cindy's gift to Kathi's memory was in the form of a verse which she wrote in anguish one night. She called it "For Every Sister."

Tomorrow,
I'll try to understand her,
Try to understand the excitement behind
Those piercing black eyes,
Try to understand her zeal for life,
Tireless energy, and love for others.
Tomorrow,
I'll sit down beside her and get to know
This sister of mine.
I'll get to know the skinny little girl
I grew up with and shared a bedroom with
For all our teen years.
Tomorrow,
We'll share secrets together,
We'll go for a long walk,
We'll just sit together for hours and laugh.
Tomorrow,
I'll ask her about her boyfriends,
I'll ask her about her girlfriends,
I'll even ask what her favorite subject is in school.
Today?
I'm too busy,
I have too much to do,
She's getting on my nerves.
Today,

111

She's borrowing my precious clothes, ruining them.
Today,
She's using up all the gas in my car.
Today,
She's asking stupid questions
I just don't feel like answering.
Today,
I'm too tired.
But tomorrow,
I'll tell her how much I love her,
I'll hug her and tell her she's pretty,
I'll tell her I'm glad I have a sister . . . tomorrow.
Tomorrow
Has finally come and she is gone!

A task I had been postponing loomed before me — going through Kathi's clothing and belongings. I held each dress closely to me, remembering vividly some occasion when she had worn each particular outfit. As I was alone, I let the tears flow without restraint, lovingly folding the familiar red and white cheerleading sweater. I packed box after box, but I put the "Angel Dress" back in the closet; I couldn't part with it. The little green blouse which we had purchased that day together — the only piece of her clothing found at the accident scene — was also folded and put away.

While going through her desk, I found a folded piece of paper at the very bottom of the drawer. It was a poem Kathi had written when she was sixteen — a poem which revealed the heart of Kathi.

The Wonders of God

Looking all about me,
It's very plain to see
That God created everything,
The birds, the sky, the trees.
But then I look around some more
To the painful side of life,
At Satan, who tries to o'er power the world,
Lead people into strife;

The madness all about me
That seems to prevail,
The devil's really working,
But God can never fail.
For on Calvary's cross He died,
To save me from my sin,
So that forever after
I may enter in.
Oh, thank You, my dear Lord,
For setting me free.
I'm saved forever after,
Now I'll serve and live for Thee!

Honors were bestowed upon Kathi, Mike, and John.
Memorial trophies were set up at their high schools and
places of work. And these tributes were a continual re-
minder of what lives surrendered to God can do.

That fall Cleveland High dedicated the Homecoming
game to Kathi, and *Impact* ran a story about them, telling
of their last week at camp.

Marilee Drown, a camper from Arizona, penned these
lines when she heard of the accident:

The impact of metal against metal.
. . . shattered glass
. . . sirens . . .
lifeless youth. . . .
In the darkness
the gaping emptiness of death!
LORD!
. . . WHY?
Yet, *always*
in the darkness
the gaping emptiness of death
. . . of lifeless youth.
The impact of death without remedy
. . . shatters hearts of the living.
PLEASE
bring the remedy for death to lifeless youth yet living.

113

This became our daily prayer — that God would use our daughter's life and death to His glory — that many lifeless teen-agers would find life in Him.

Our prayers have been answered. We have seen it happen!

The Wallis family has seen it happen!

The Quatro family has seen it happen!

And Dave, back in Brazil, testifying continually to God's miraculous healing, has seen it happen!

23

FRIDAY, MARCH 13 — Kathi would have been nineteen.

Memories of past slumber parties came to mind. No empty Coke bottles or wall-to-wall potato chips this year.

A small bouquet of flowers arrived from Dave and Ethel Wallis in memory of her birthday.

Although six months had gone by, pain was my constant companion; although we had seen miracle after miracle and experienced the peace and grace of God, this day brought a different kind of sorrow. For this was my daughter's special day — nineteen years ago I had given her life.

That evening we drove to my mother's home for dinner. It was my cousin's birthday too, and I wondered if I could say "happy birthday" without crying. Eighteen years ago he had given Kathi a tiny locket for her first birthday — for the girl who shared his special day.

Through the waves of memory of that night, I am reminded again of the brevity of life. For my brother Leo had only nine more months to live; my strong brother would die suddenly, unexpectedly, and would enter heaven's gates to greet his Lord, his dad, his younger brother, and his niece.

And only one month after we buried my brother, Kathi's friend Jim — "special" Jim — died in an accident. As I stood at the back of the church at Jim's funeral, I remembered him weeping so openly as he helped carry Kathi's coffin. I remembered him throwing stones at her window and their long talks at midnight. He had said at the graveside, "Kathi taught me so much."

Once again Glen, Tom, and Jon picked up a coffin and set it beside a freshly dug grave.

"The Lord is picking," Glen said quietly.

One year from the date of the September accident, our family, with Ethel Wallis, Steve Quatro, Ethel Emily Wallis, and Debby, drove to the cemetery to lay flowers on the graves. When we arrived, we found two teen-age girls sitting beside the graves; they had gone to school with Kathi.

"If it wasn't for Kathi," Mary Ann said, in the course of our conversation, "I wouldn't have my Savior."

The caretaker who was standing nearby began speaking to us in broken English, finally resorting to his native Spanish. Ethel Emily, who was a veteran missionary to Mexico, walked over and began talking with him.

"He wanted to say," Ethel told us, "that he wondered about these three graves. He said he was here the day of the funeral and that there has been someone here nearly every day since to lay flowers or say a prayer. He wanted to know the story behind the three plots."

And Ethel told him the story of Kathi, Mike, and John.

Thus, a day that I had dreaded became a healing benediction to our daughter's staunch testimony.

Our second Christmas without Kathi the Lord filled our longing hearts with His love and joy. Tom called to wish us "a Merry Christmas"; Bev stopped by to bring us a beautiful poinsettia plant and we talked of our wonderful Lord. She was growing spiritually, making her witness felt at college and among her friends. And Debby, now in the Waves and home on furlough, spent all Christmas Eve with us.

116

"I want to be a missionary," she told me when we were alone in the quiet living room.

My eyes filled with tears as I remembered a confused, troubled Debby sobbing her heart out at our home after Kathi's funeral — a girl who had tried everything to find peace found it at last in the Prince of Peace Himself.

My eyes were drawn to Kathi's always-smiling picture on the wall.

"I'm out for the world," she had said. "No time to waste." And she had reached the world — the world which God had put her into — her world of teen-agers. Her world of Bev, Felicia, Sharon, Hope, Debby, Steve, Janie, Jim, Glen, and the list goes on and on. . . .

I see her clearly now — long hair flying in the wind, bare feet, and blue jeans — our carefree, laughing Kathi. Kathi, who could whisper honestly, "I, too, would be willing to die if it would bring my friends to Christ."

I see the little red Mustang traveling bravely through the mountains carrying four young people, laughing, singing, talking, praying, planning — and in an instant three are home.

Home free for all eternity.